MAINSTREAMING THE LEARNING DISABLED ADOLESCENT

A Manual of Strategies and Materials

Dolores M. Woodward, Ph.D.

AN ASPEN PUBLICATION®
Aspen Systems Corporation
Rockville, Maryland
London
1981

Library of Congress Cataloging in Publication Data

Woodward, Dolores M.
Mainstreaming the learning disabled adolescent.

Includes index.
1. Learning disabilities. 2. Mainstreaming
in education. 3. Adolescence. I. Title.
LC4704.W66   371.9   80-19566
ISBN: 0-89443-299-0

Library of Congress Catalog Card Number: 80-19566
ISBN: 0-89443-299-0

Printed in the United States of America

1 2 3 4 5

To My Daughters,
Kim and Rebecca

To My Parents,
Ralph and Rose Coppola

Most of all,
To My Husband,
Beaven

whose support, understanding, and patience
enabled me to complete this work.

Table of Contents

Preface

I have always felt that the true textbook for the pupil is his teacher.
Mahatma Gandhi

Learning disabilities have been called the "invisible" handicap. Students who are learning-disabled (hereafter referred to as "LD" students) suffer from a disorder in one or more of the basic psychological processes involved in understanding or using spoken or written language. These psychological disorders can be manifested in disorders of listening, thinking, talking, reading, writing, spelling, or arithmetic.

Many adolescents who have experienced frustration and anxiety in school because of learning disabilities develop emotional problems as a result. These students' motivations, interests, and learning capacities are also influenced, of course, by the tasks and demands of adolescence itself. Peer influence is a significant factor in their lives. Within a mainstream setting (i.e., within regular classes), the teacher must address the need for peer comparison and concomitant self-evaluation, as well as addressing each student's learning disability.

The LD adolescent's expanded academic experiences—in addition to his increased personal and social activities—make the task of effective intervention a difficult one.

This book is a comprehensive reservoir of strategies, activities, methods, and resources that will enable the regular-education teacher not only to survive with LD students in his mainstream classes, but also—and more significantly—his students will experience academic and social success in the mainstream setting.

Dolores M. Woodward

Note: This book follows the standard practice of using a "masculine" pronoun wherever the pronoun refers to both males and females. "Feminine" pronouns appear only where antecedents are exclusively female.

ix

Acknowledgments

I wish to thank the many graduate students in my courses whose ideas, interests, and studies contributed to this work. My special thanks go to Mark Mathieu, Barbara Santamaria, Betty Utz, Maxine Margolis, and Buzzina White.

I owe a special debt of gratitude to Gini Chuck, who typed the manuscript for publication.

Introduction

Since its enactment in 1975, the "Education for All Handicapped Children Act" (P.L. 94-142) has had a dramatic impact in the field of education. Adolescents in traditional classrooms are being identified as "exceptional," and thus are also receiving special services. Those students who were previously labeled "exceptional," and were receiving services only in segregated classrooms or resource rooms, are now joining integrated classrooms. School systems are urgently seeking to comply with the Handicapped Act's directive "to educate special students in the least restrictive setting."

Schools still face great difficulties in developing appropriate mainstream programs for LD adolescents. The difficulty of integrating special students in traditional classrooms is compounded by the existence of separate, compartmentalized training for special and regular educators—which allows little sharing of expertise between the two groups.

Regular, "mainstream" educators who suddenly find themselves responsible for "exceptional" students have asked for a survival guide which will assist them in their day-to-day work. This book provides a collection of pragmatic and proven interventions, techniques, and approaches for secondary-level educators.

It should be used as a vehicle for developing liaison between regular teachers, who are often unwilling to admit their feelings of inadequacy with special students, and special educators, who are often hesitant to admit their unfamiliarity with secondary-level academic subjects.

It addresses a need that has received little attention to date—the need to develop individualized academic programs to meet the individual needs of the mainstreamed LD adolescent. It is applicable for use by junior- and senior-high-school teachers in all subject areas, as well as by special-education consultants working with those teachers.

Unlike other publications in the field, it is built upon five years of experience, and addresses those concerns which teachers themselves have identified as priority issues. It is a direct response to the identified needs of professionals in the field.

A second advantage is its unified, pragmatic approach. The step-by-step format means that it can be used effectively by professionals of very diverse training and experience.

Its comprehensiveness makes it a must for every educator's professional library. It covers the educational programming gamut, from "How to Get the Most for Your Money in Buying Materials" (a concern for most teachers who work with limited budgets) to "How to Be a More Effective Communicator."

It is intended for direct application in any secondary-school classroom by any educator responsible for providing instruction to mainstreamed LD students. Its suggestions can, in addition, improve the education of "regular" students.

It focuses on *observable* learning problems, and provides *proven* suggestions on how to remedy each student's learning difficulties. Special-education jargon is avoided wherever possible, thereby enhancing its attractiveness to the regular educator.

Extensive lists of references and materials (which follow each section) allow the professional reader to investigate further any topic of special interest.

The format reflects my philosophy: education is most effective when it is structured, paced, sequenced, and individualized!

Chapter 1

Creating a Climate for Learning in the Mainstream

1

CREATING A CLIMATE FOR LEARNING

The effectiveness of a teacher of mainstreamed LD adolescents is contingent on many factors. Of major significance are the teacher's underlying attitudes and beliefs regarding the education of exceptional adolescents.

Traditional teacher-training programs have reinforced the notion that there exists a definitive set of rules that must be carefully followed to ensure an effective teaching/learning experience. In contrast, special-education teachers have been trained from a philosophical base that is diametrically opposed to the "sacredness" of these "truths."

One observable conflict in most mainstream classrooms occurs when teachers who were reared on a philosophy of conformity in education attempt to teach LD students who, as research has proven, benefit most from an individualized teaching strategy. The pervasiveness of this phenomenon is more readily apparent through a contrast of regular-education principles with those of special education.

Regular- vs. Special-Education Principles of Learning

Situational and Temporal Learning

Regular-education: "Learning" takes place primarily while school is in session.

Special-education: Each student should be individually tested to determine (1) the time during which his maximum learning can take place, and (2) where this learning should occur.

Responsible Agent in the Learning Process

Regular-education: The teacher holds the primary responsibility for the amount of learning which takes place.

Special-education: Learning is a direct result of the interaction of objectives, strategies, and materials derived from students, parents, teachers, and related services providers.

Instructional Medium

Regular-education: The teacher's job is to fill the "empty child vessel" with information through verbal presentation.

Special-education: The manner in which material may be presented most effectively to a student must be determined on an individual basis. There is no uniformly "best" method of instruction—only that which is best for the specific student in question.

The Lock-step Nature of Learning

Regular-education: A classroom of students can learn the same content in the same time. This is particularly true of "regular" classes on the secondary level, in which the emphasis is more on content than at the elementary level.

Special-education: Students' existing levels of development and rates of learning must be individually determined. The content to be presented to each student is contingent upon his level of cognitive, affective, and psychomotor functioning.

Teacher Autonomy

Regular-education: A teacher is "in charge of" and responsible for his students, and it is he who knows what is best for them.

Special-education: A child is a complex being. Instruction, to be most effective, must be directed at the "total child." This goal is achieved through an interdisciplinary, collaborative effort: the classroom teacher is only one of several agents in the decision-making process affecting the student's learning.

Learning Atmosphere

Regular-education: The best school is a quiet school; the best student is the one who is quietly absorbed in the assigned task.

Special-education: Effective learning may assume a variety of forms and be the product of many different methods. Silence may indicate nothing more than boredom or frustration.

Student Concentration

Regular-education: All children are capable of learning provided they attend to and concentrate on the task the teacher has presented.

Special-education: Before a child can learn, the teacher must determine his capacity for attention and the conditions in which his attention is enhanced. Concentration is a function of many variables, and should be viewed as a separate phenomenon in the learning process.

What are the factors responsible for a child's academic success? Kuhlen (1952) argues that there are many. "Achievement is, of course, the result of many factors." One must consider the student's motivation and interest in the task at hand. These two factors often are reflected in the amount of energy that is invested into the task completion. The most obvious factors that contribute to student success are the innate abilities he possesses: his intelligence, stamina, health, physical resiliency, and general emotional well-being. Of equal importance are the factors which are less easily identifiable. The student's value system, his cultural heritage and self-esteem constitute but a few of the many factors that would fall into this category. For the LD student, achievement is frequently not in proportion to the effort he expends on the task. Poor grades, frustration, and little inherent positive reinforcement in academic tasks are ancillary factors that weigh against academic achievement for the LD adolescent. Over a sustained period of time the result is a student who becomes "turned off" to the educational process itself.

Teaching Style in the Classroom

Regular-education: Effectiveness with a class of students is dependent on the teacher's ability as a performer who can maintain student interest and involvement via a personal teaching style.

Special-education: There is no "best" teaching style. With some exceptional students, the teacher who simply engineers the environment for the student to learn independently is most effective; for others, "peer tutoring" is the most effective instructional method.

"Panacea" Teaching Methods

Regular-education: A teacher's effectiveness is a matter of selecting the "right" material to use with a specific class or student.

Special-education: There are no special teaching methods or materials that are appropriate for all exceptional children. Appropriateness of method or material is determined by what is best for a particular child at a particular time.

Normative- vs. Criterion-Referenced Teaching

Regular-education: The "deficit feedback model" is employed. Herein, the teacher tells the student where his performance is inadequate: on tests, by marking the student's incorrect responses; on report cards, by letting the student know how well he performed compared to his peers by rank-ordering all students in the class (i.e., a normative-referenced model).

Special-education: The student's performance is evaluated on a "criterion base" relative to his acquisition of, or demonstrated competence with, a specific skill (as stated in a behavioral objective). The student is informed of his performance relative to the task itself, not relative to the performance of his peers.

These ten incongruities between the special- and regular-education emphases serve to make program development difficult when both approaches are integrated in mainstream situations.

WHAT WE KNOW ABOUT LEARNING

Research has clearly revealed a number of educational truisms. Watson (1963) published a list of principles summarizing what we know about learning. The principles have been further validated through recent research conducted in the area of operant conditioning.

The following principles are derived from the behaviorists' research.

1. Behavior is learned and maintained by the consequences that behavior evokes from its environment.

This law suggests that behaviors which are rewarded have a high probability of recurring. Further, it suggests that behavior an individual found satisfying or successful in previous situations will tend to be repeated. A teacher designing a plan for an LD student should thus provide for a steady cumulative sequence of successful behaviors.

2. The value of a reward is in direct proportion to its immediacy of presentation following the student's behavior, i.e., the more closely timed the reward is to a behavior, the greater is its reinforcing value.

Programmed self-instruction is an effective instructional method primarily because it provides feedback to the student almost immediately after his performance.

3. Feedback, as an ongoing facet of instruction, is an effective learning enhancer.

A student's achievements are the result of a teacher's "shaping" a desired response. This suggests that the teacher reward successive approximations of the student's performance toward the desired goal.

4. Before learning can take place there must be a state of "readiness" on the part of the student. This state is a function of many factors. Important considerations are: the student's physiological and psychological maturity, his mastery of prerequisite skills, and a learning environment which is conducive to growth and is facilitative in design.

5. The use of intimidation, threat, and punishment are questionable as learning "prods." Research has shown that their effects upon a student are mixed. Frequently, negative side effects result because the student associates the punishment with the individual dispensing the punishment. If the dispenser is the teacher, the potential effectiveness of instruction is greatly attenuated through the negative feelings engendered. In addition, punishment does not facilitate the student finding the correct response and therefore does not have a constructive net effect upon the student.

6. One of the most effective learning situations is one which provides the student with an opportunity for a novel and stimulating experience. In fact, this has been repeatedly shown to be as effective as rewards or reinforcements that gratify physical desires. Teachers should consider using this principle in situations where the class appears to have reached an interest plateau or when presenting material which will necessitate drill.

7. It is essential that the teacher establish an appropriate level of challenge for the LD student as it has been proven that the most effective effort is put forth when there is "a probable but not certain" chance of success with the task.

8. Students' enthusiasm and participation are increased if they, themselves, have actively been involved in the selection and design of the project they are to study. This principle is of particular relevance to the adolescent for whom active participation is a salient learning facet.

9. Learning occurs when student decision making is possible. If the activity is overly teacher directed, the result will be student apathy or mechanical conformity in many instances. Independent behavior is an essential learning goal for the LD adolescent.

10. Criticism and failure are antithetical to learning. Self-esteem is very much a situational phenomenon. If an adolescent believes that his role as a student has little value, he tends to seek his role of importance outside school. He is also likely to develop feelings of resentment toward teachers, books, and school.

11. When the failure experiences continue for any extended period of time or if the failure is frequent, the result is student behavior which is often characterized by lack of purpose and lack of integration. LD adolescents, who have often had little success in an academic setting, tend to be inattentive, poorly motivated to learn, and frequently angry.

12. Students learn more from material they have read if they spend the time recalling what they have read than by rereading the material. This principle is a very important consideration for the LD adolescent with memory deficits. The

teacher may suggest the student use a tape recorder or note in writing the main points in the material.

13. It has been well documented that individuals tend to remember new information which conforms to their previous attitudes. For the LD adolescent, this suggests that of equal significance to the content to be presented to the adolescent is the manner in which it is presented.

14. Recall of new learning is facilitated if the learning takes place in a context similar to that in which it is to be used. Teaching the LD adolescent consumerism, for example, in a real life retail situation is far more effective than to attempt to teach this in a classroom in the abstract.

15. Achievement is very reinforcing to the learner. The student's sense of satisfaction with the attainment of success or accomplishment generalizes to life situations outside the classroom. This suggests that a learner's satisfaction with his own achievements has a high value for further learning.

16. Forgetting proceeds rapidly at first, then more and more slowly. The opportunity to recall the information shortly after learning reduces the amount forgotten. For the teacher, this suggests that review shortly after initial learning is an effective strategy. Practice at gradually increasing intervals facilitates long-term retention.

LEARNING DISABILITIES: A DEFINITION

The definition of "specific learning disability" as it occurs in the adolescent is usually predicated upon the definition offered by the National Advisory Committee on Handicapped Children (1968). This definition suggests that three criteria, paraphrased below, be considered in viewing school-age populations.

1. There must be a significant discrepancy between a child's potential to achieve academic success (innate potential and abilities) and his demonstrated grade-level achievement. This dictates that a reading of potential be obtained through some type of standardized test. The Weschler Intelligence Scale and Stanford-Binet are the two such tests most often employed. Grade-achievement can be determined by administering one of the many group and individual tests that have been developed. (Refer to Appendix E.)
2. The disparity between ability and achievement is due to a disturbance involving some basic psychological process.
3. The learning problems cannot be caused directly by such conditions as deprivation, blindness, or mental retardation. This criterion is often called the "exclusion clause."

CHARACTERISTICS OF LD ADOLESCENTS AND IMPLICATIONS FOR INSTRUCTION

The task of delineating variables that accurately characterize LD students is both complex and tedious. A study of students who have been identified as learning-disabled reveals some common characteristics:

- *Inadequate acquisition of basic skills.* This deficiency is frequently ignored by the secondary school, which focuses on the delivery of content. This characteristic of the LD student suggests that there should be remedial work in basic skill areas.

- *Peak/valley learning profile.* When one examines an LD adolescent's learning abilities and proficiencies in different subject areas, one consistently observes that he has certain strengths and certain weaknesses. If one focuses on remediating an LD student's weak areas, he may fail to make adequate progress in his areas of strength. This suggests that those responsible for developing programs for LD students must keep both remediation and continuing instruction in perspective.

- *Deficient learning-related skills.* It is essential that secondary-level students have comprehension skills and vocabulary that are adequate to cope with the concepts and vocabulary of the secondary-level curriculum. An ability frequently overlooked—but essential for successful functioning—is the ability to perform quickly within the secondary-level classroom. This characteristic suggests that a teacher should analyze his lesson plans to determine which related skills are required of his adolescent students.

- *Inadequate listening skills.* The most prevalent method of presenting material to students in secondary-level classrooms is the lecture. For a student to succeed with a secondary curriculum, he must be able to understand sentences, remember what is spoken, follow directions, recall ideas, etc. Instruction should thus include programs aimed at developing these skills.

- *Inadequate internal structure.* Students who are dependent on external structure to guide their performance often find themselves at a loss in secondary schools, where teachers tend to require a good deal of independence from students. It is important that a teacher continue to provide each LD student with organization and support in the assigned learning tasks.

- *Social and personal problems.* These problems include a low self-concept, difficulties with personal relationships, poor social judgments, and poor social perceptions. LD students experience social difficulties because of their inability to generalize from one situation to similar situations, their lack of flexibility, their extreme sensitivity, and their difficulty in interpreting the mood of those around them. A teacher should include counseling sessions, group experiences, and specific discussion directed toward these areas in his instruction.

- *Perceptual deficiencies.* Perception is the process of organizing or interpreting the raw data obtained through the senses. LD students often experience processing irregularities.

Given the complexity of the LD adolescent population, it is difficult to prescribe methodologies and interventions without systematic research. This research is facilitated if it is guided by a framework which enables both a unified and systematic approach.

Programs at the secondary level should be predicated upon the psychoeducational characteristics of LD adolescents.

WHO IS THE LD STUDENT?

A project sponsored by the Easter Seal Research Foundation of the National Society for Crippled Children and Adults, Inc., and the National Institute for Neurological Diseases and Blindness attempted to isolate the distinguishing characteristics of LD students. After reviewing more than 100 publications, they produced a document (NINDB Monograph No. 3, coordinated by Dr. Sam D. Clements, from the U.S. Department of Health, Education and Welfare) which reveals the following characteristic symptoms and signs:

1. irregular, spotty test-performance indicators
2. impairments of perception and concept formation
3. specific neurological indicators
4. disorders of speech and communication
5. disorders of motor function
6. academic achievement and adjustment (variability in performance; disability in specific subject areas such as math, reading, and spelling; poor organizational ability; frequent confusion)
7. disorders of thinking processes (poor ability for abstract reasoning and concrete thinking)
8. physical characteristics (developmentally immature for age)
9. emotional characteristics (poor emotional and impulse control, low frustration tolerance)
10. inadequate interpersonal capacities

11. sleep characteristics (excessive movement during sleep, irregular sleep patterns)
12. variations in physical development (frequent lags in developmental milestones, physically immature)
13. characteristics of social behavior (social incompetence, inappropriate behavior for situation)
14. variations of personality (excessive sensitivity, excessive mood variation, poor adjustment to environmental changes)
15. disorders of attention and concentration (short attention span for age, limited concentration ability, impaired ability to make decisions, overly distractible for age)

These are the ten characteristics most often cited by various authors, in order of their frequency:

1. hyperactivity
2. perceptual motor impairments
3. emotional ability
4. general coordination deficiencies
5. disorders of attention (short attention span, distractibility), perseveration
6. impulsivity
7. disorders of memory and thinking
8. specific learning disabilities in reading, arithmetic, writing, and spelling
9. disorders of speech and hearing
10. equivocal neurological signs and electroencephalographic irregularities

The "signs" approach above can serve *only* as a guideline for the purpose of identification and diagnosis.

The clear conclusion revealed by this approach is that learning disbilities are extraordinarily variable.

Characteristics of the LD Adolescent

With the LD adolescent, the "signs" can become contaminated and masked by the student's age and his years in the educational system, and most significantly by the adolescent stage of development itself. It is important to look at the adolescent as a separate entity.

The Unique Adolescent

The longer an LD adolescent functions within the educational system, the greater is his "uniqueness." This suggests that teachers must use caution in attempting to generalize from the individual LD adolescent to the group of adolescent students.

The Independent Adolescent

One of the most important tasks that adolescents face is to assume their independence. This suggests that educators, in designing remedial or compensatory programs for LD adolescents, must actively involve those students in the design planning. To do otherwise immediately creates student resistance and serves to attenuate the possible effectiveness of the plan.

Developmental Tasks of Adolescence

There are specific tasks that the adolescent must accomplish to facilitate his present and future adjustment.
The tasks are:

1. To prepare for an economic career. This is essential if the adolescent is to maintain an independent life style.
2. To achieve success in one's male or female social role and in this role to behave in a socially responsible manner.
3. To achieve emotional independence from the adult society. This includes both parents and other significant adults in the adolescent's life.
4. To prepare for marriage and family life through achieving mature relations with male and female peers.
5. To acquire stable systems of values, ethics, and other principles needed to guide mature behavior.

Havinghurst (1972) is an excellent reference for additional reading in this area.

The Mobile Adolescent

It is accepted, on the elementary-school level, that neither "all learning" nor the "most effective learning" takes place within classroom walls; this principle is even more valid for the adolescent. Educators who are attempting to design programs should consider the adolescent's increased mobility and the potential this mobility affords for a broader continuum of learning environments.

The Career/Vocationally-Oriented Adolescent

Adolescence is the time when a student must begin to make occupational and life decisions. The turbulence of adolescence makes this tentative decision making a most difficult endeavor for regular-education adolescents; for the LD adolescent, it may appear catastrophic! Educators must begin to mesh life goals with academic/ curriculum goals if they are to ensure an appropriate education for the secondary LD student.

A teacher must be cognizant of the LD adolescent's need to learn *explicitly* the skills and knowledge that might be acquired *inferentially* by the regular-education student. Appropriate curriculum activities for LD adolescents might include such courses as "How to Make a Decision" and "The Steps in Establishing Priorities."

The Emotional Adolescent

The emotional and behavioral problems that often accompany the learning disability of a student become more obvious in adolescence. Faced with increased educational demands, with pressure to make decisions that have long-term ramifications, and with the prospect of a few more years in the system, many adolescents despair and drop out. It is essential that a secondary-level educator be cognizant of this aspect of learning disabilities, and that he address both the affective areas of the educational process and the cognitive dimensions of learning; otherwise, the LD adolescent will not be effectively maintained within the mainstream.

Learning Disability and Personality

It is difficult to determine the precise effects of a learning disability on an adolescent's personality. Authors who emphasize the emotional and personality difficulties that accompany the learning problems of the LD student are on the increase as our ability and commitment to identify and label LD students improve.

The LD adolescent is the product of many years of repeated academic failure and frustration, which often result in a poor self-concept and a concomitant development of elaborate defenses. The LD student often interprets his failures as indications of limited intelligence—although the reality is that an adolescent must possess at least average intelligence before he can be classified as "learning-disabled."

The LD adolescent may, in fact, suffer an identity crisis as a result of feelings of inadequacy. He may ask himself: "What is my place in the world of education?"

These very real concerns, which affect the adolescent's functioning, should be considered when teachers design a curriculum to meet the LD adolescent's needs. For example, if an adolescent is coping with real and immediate questions of identity—"What am I going to become?" or "How will I survive?"—he will find it difficult to appreciate a lesson on the nuances of English composition.

The cumulative effects of persistent academic failure mean that LD adolescents often manifest a greater fear than their "normal" adolescent counterparts. LD students are often so discouraged that they will not even attempt academically-related tasks.

The teacher responsible for educating an LD adolescent must attempt to understand the difficulties he is experiencing as a result of his disability, and then must relate this understanding to the classroom. This would suggest, for example, that educational programs for these students should include specific instruction on communication and interaction skills. Teachers should not assume that inferential learning about social situations will occur. The nature of the LD student dictates that he be guided to an understanding of interpersonal dynamics through concrete, direct, and sequential instruction.

PRINCIPLES OF DIAGNOSIS

In order to determine what and how to teach the LD adolescent, it is important that both the regular- and the special-educator understand the diagnostic-prescriptive model of educational evaluation.

"Diagnosis" is simply defined as an inference derived from a student's performance. Two factors must be assessed: the student's present level of functioning and the manner of his performance.

In diagnosing a student's learning state, the person responsible for "testing" seeks answers to the following questions: What is the nature of the student's learning problem? What factors are responsible for the existence of the learning deficiency? What is the most appropriate plan to ameliorate the present problem?

Principle 1. *Each student is a unique learner.*
Diagnosis begins with an assessment of the individual student as a person with unique instructional needs. Essential questions include:

• What is the student able to do?

• What area(s) of difficulty is he encountering?

• What factors are causing the student's learning difficulties?

• What efforts to remediate the student's learning deficiencies are viable?

This principle asks that the teacher employ a variety of reference points in determining the individual student's learning profile. Three major reference areas the teacher should explore are:

1. Developmental reference. What tasks is the child required and expected to perform with proficiency at different age levels?

2. Cognitive reference. What is the hierarchy of skills within a task?
3. Affective reference. What is the effect of the student's emotional level on his ability to perform cognitive tasks.

Principle 2. *Diagnosis is a cyclical process.*
Diagnosis implies, first, pre-testing to determine the child's level of proficiency with a particular skill. The next step is to teach the skill, employing that method which is determined to be most effective for the child in question. The final step is a postinstructional test to determine how much learning has occurred.
Diagnosis must focus on:

1. incremental learning in a sequential hierarchy
2. specific objective-setting
3. specific behavioral responses expected from the student

Principle 3. *The goal of diagnosis is an educational plan.*
The product of diagnosis is an educational plan that includes appropriate methods for remediating the student's areas of disability. It should not attempt to determine the etiology of the disability. Without a prescriptive plan of instruction, diagnosis is analogous to half an equation: it can go nowhere, and it has no inherent value.

Principle 4. *The most effective diagnosis takes place within a life-context.*
The most meaningful diagnosis often occurs in the environment where the student is to demonstrate the skill. As such, each adult who interacts with the student within the educational setting is able to contribute to the diagnosis through observations and individual behavioral ratings of the student. For example, it is preferable to measure "attending to task" behavior in the classroom—and with real tasks—than to measure it with a standardized test in the office of the school psychologist.
A student's learning problem often has *multiple* causes. In interpreting test results, the teacher should delineate the student's strengths *and* weaknesses as a learner. By incorporating the student's learning strengths in his diagnosis, the teacher can develop a balanced educational prescription—one in which the student's successes in his areas of strength will motivate him to persevere with tasks that are more frustrating for him.

Principle 5. *The appropriateness of a diagnosis is a function of the diversity and number of assessments undertaken.*

HOW TO CONDUCT A DIAGNOSIS

Step 1. The teacher's first task in diagnosing an LD adolescent's learning problem is to conduct an overall screening. The student's *expected* level of functioning must be compared with his *actual* performance. (Expectation is a function of the student's intellectual potential, as revealed by some indicator of the student's ability to achieve.) Personal data in the student's record should be reviewed.

Step 2. The information collected during the overall screening must be compared with the student's actual functional level as determined by less formal assessment. This step is called the "survey diagnosis " and consists primarily of classroom screening and observation.

Note that a current major educational issue is that of accountability for instructional effectiveness. Collecting behavioral observations is one way a teacher can contribute to the development of improved, experience-based programs for the LD adolescent. Observing student behavior at different times of the academic day, in different classroom situations, with different teachers, and with different subjects may produce significant diagnostic information.

Step 3. The teacher's third task is to describe the student's specific learning disability. The teacher should now attend to such specifics as the student's knowledge and his proficiency with particular skills. It is important to recognize the need to supplement formal testing with informal observations. This phase of diagnosis is identified with an individualized assessment of performance.

Step 4. Intensive diagnosis comes next. The teacher begins to develop an analysis of the factors causing the disability.

Step 5. The final step in the diagnostic process is to design a program of educational remediation predicated upon an analysis of the information produced during earlier stages of the diagnosis.

LEARNING STYLES

One purpose of a student diagnosis is to identify that student's learning style. Several guides have been published that teachers may use to direct their observations. One helpful guide is shown in Exhibit 1-1.

Exhibit 1-1 Observation Sheet To Determine Student Learning Style

1. Does the student assume responsibility for his own education?
   ___ never   ___ sometimes   ___ often

2. Does the student's participation differ from group to individual situations?
   ___ never   ___ sometimes   ___ often

3. Does the student exhibit flexibility in accepting change?
   ___ never   ___ sometimes   ___ often

4. Does the student maintain involvement with the task?
   ___ never   ___ sometimes   ___ often

5. Does the student monitor his performance?
   ___ never   ___ sometimes   ___ often

6. Does the student frustrate easily?
   ___ never   ___ sometimes   ___ often

7. Does the student require frequent encouragement?
   ___ never   ___ sometimes   ___ often

8. Does there appear to be a significant difference between the student's ability to concentrate on verbal activities and his ability to concentrate on visual activities?
   ___ never   ___ sometimes   ___ often

9. Does there appear to be a student preference for communicating with gestures as opposed to communication through language?
   ___ never   ___ sometimes   ___ often

10. Does there appear to be a consistent approach to problem solving?
    ___ never   ___ sometimes   ___ often

DIAGNOSIS: A MODEL

In diagnosing a student's learning style, a teacher should aim to delineate not only the student's deficiencies and learning disabilities, but also his learning strengths.

Tests

Competent and comprehensive diagnosis requires that the examiner possess specific competence with tests, procedures, and forms that is acquired through actual interaction with the student being evaluated. These requirements follow. The examiner must be conversant with tests used to determine the student's academic functioning levels, disability area, specific skills and a student's strengths and weaknesses as a learner.

Procedures

1. The first assessment is usually of the student's potential for academic success. This is known traditionally as an Intelligence Quotient (I.Q.) determination.

2. The next essential step is to ascertain the student's actual academic attainments. This measurement is made with a standardized achievement test.

3. The evaluator then compares the student's potential for success with his actual functioning. Significant discrepancies are then examined for indications of their cause(s). For example, a student with an I.Q. of 100—that is, an average I.Q.—would generally be expected in third grade to be functioning in academics at a third-grade level. A student of average I.Q. whose achievement falls short of this expectation—for example, a third-grade student who is functioning on a first-grade level—indicates that other factors must be examined further.

4. Sensory processing is evaluated. The evaluator measures the student's capacity to learn through a verbal mode, an auditory mode, a sensory-integrated mode, and a motor mode.

5. The student's degree of mastery of requisite skills necessary for successful functioning within the grade level he is placed is important data to be gathered in any evaluation undertaken.

The Student Profile

The educator responsible for prescribing appropriate learning experiences for the LD adolescent should then prepare a student profile of educational strengths and weaknesses. It is essential to incorporate all data derived earlier in the diagnostic process—both formal and informal—as outlined below:

Profile

Strengths	*Weaknesses*
Average I.Q.	Deficient fine-motor skills
Perseverance to task	Auditory reception
Visual memory	Sequential memory

Note that the outline above reflects only a partial profile. Using only those strengths and weaknesses listed, however, the teacher would know that:

1. Writing should be minimized as a learning requirement, owing to the student's poor fine-motor skills. Allowing the student to use a prepared guide, or a tape recorder to take notes, is suggested.
2. The student's strong visual memory suggests the desirability of using a visual approach to present new terminology, etc.
3. Sequential memory deficits indicate the need to keep directions short, simplify the language used, etc.
4. The student's perseverance to assigned tasks indicates that motivation is a factor that may be used in sustaining his interest.

The Prescription

Teachers are well-advised to set both long-term and short-term educational goals for each student. The student should be an active contributor to the goal-setting process.

"INDIVIDUALLY GUIDED EDUCATION" LEARNING STYLES

One of the suggested guides to view a student's learning style was developed by the staff of Wilson Elementary School in Janesville, Wisconsin. This group, which piloted the development of "Individually Guided Education (IGE)," developed the following list of student learning styles.

Incremental learner. This student is the "bricklayer." He prefers step-by-step learning, and tends to work well independently.

Teacher response: Break down learning tasks into small, discrete increments, and present the information in a carefully paced manner. The teacher's role is that of an educational engineer.

Intuitive learner. This student "leaps to broad generalizations." Often the quality of his thinking outpaces his skill in verbalizing knowledge.

Teacher response: Allow the student to express his knowledge in an other-than-verbal way.

Sensory specialist. This student uses a multisensory approach to learning. One sense is combined with another to enhance learning (sight with hearing, for example). Often this student is hypersensitive to stimuli within his environment.

Teacher response: Shelter the student from overstimulation through the use of a study carrel. This will cut down the degree of distractions within the classroom.

Emotionally involved learner. This is the student who learns best when he has an established relationship with his teacher.

Teacher response: Provide frequent and personal feedback to the student about his performance. Teacher attention for student's maintenance of effort with an assigned task is very reinforcing (rewarding) to this type of student.

Emotionally neutral learner. This student prefers a learning situation where objectives are clear. The student's interpersonal relationships are more subdued than those of the average student.

Teacher response: Contracting with the student for specific learning performance.

Eclectic learner. This student is very rare among the LD student population, as he can adapt to any learning situation.

Teacher response: It may be useful to determine this student's preferred learning style. In diagnosing "how the student is best able to learn," it is important to consider the environmental factors which affect the student as well as the manner in which the student "interacts" with this environment.

DIAGNOSING A STUDENT'S LEARNING STYLE: A GUIDE

1. *Time factors:*
   A. What effect does time have on the student's capacity to learn?
   B. Is there any observable difference in his productivity in a.m. versus p.m. classes?
   C. Does he fatigue quickly?
   D. Is he a slow starter?
   E. Is he able to pace his effort within a time frame?

2. *Environmental factors:*
   A. Does the student's performance improve with background music?
   B. Is the student easily drawn off task by any extraneous sound?
   C. What effect does conversation within the classroom have on his ability to concentrate?
   D. What type of seating is most conducive to the student's ability to attend—study carrel? learning corner? student desk?
   E. What effect does room temperature have upon the student's work performance?

3. *Social factors:*
   A. With what type of peer group involvement does the student appear most comfortable—small group? large group? single other peer?
   B. Does the student frequently initiate contact with teacher? with peers?
   C. Does the student's performance differ from individual to group situations?
   D. What effect do co-ed learning situations exert on the student's academic performance?
   E. How does the student's behavior differ in structured versus unstructured groups?

4. *Innate factors:*
   A. Does the student manifest an obvious sensory preference—visual? auditory?
   B. How is his performance affected through combining senses in instructional presentations?
   C. How does the student's verbal versus nonverbal performance compare—are they similar? significantly different?
   D. Does the student exhibit any "unusual" behavior in the learning situation?
   E. How does his receptive ability compare with expressive ability?

5. *Structural factors:*
   A. What type of structure elicits the most optimal student performance—fixed? variable? mutually determined?
   B. What is the student's preferred assignment type—project? contract? teacher directed tasks?
   C. What evaluative form is most reinforcing to the student—verbal? conferences? grades?
   D. How is the student motivated?
   E. How does the student deal with competition?

Most student behavior is situational (i.e., it varies with the setting). This tenet dictates that the student's educational profile must be observed within the classroom environment.

One suggested guide for focusing the teacher's observations is presented in Exhibit 1-2.

Exhibit 1-2 Behavior Observation Rating Scale

1. Student adapts easily to change of schedule and/or situation.
___ always   ___ usually   ___ sometimes   ___ seldom   ___ never

2. Student's companionship is valued by his peers.
___ always   ___ usually   ___ sometimes   ___ seldom   ___ never

3. Student becomes alarmed easily.
___ always   ___ usually   ___ sometimes   ___ seldom   ___ never

4. Student becomes upset by failure as evidenced by withdrawal.
___ always   ___ usually   ___ sometimes   ___ seldom   ___ never

5. Student hesitates to express his opinions, is extremely cautious.
___ always   ___ usually   ___ sometimes   ___ seldom   ___ never

6. Student seeks support and feedback from peers or teacher.
___ always   ___ usually   ___ sometimes   ___ seldom   ___ never

7. Student deprecates his own academic efforts.
___ always   ___ usually   ___ sometimes   ___ seldom   ___ never

8. Student manifests an appreciation of his own worth.
___ always   ___ usually   ___ sometimes   ___ seldom   ___ never

9. Student seeks attention through such behavior as speaking out of turn and making unnecessary noises.
___ always   ___ usually   ___ sometimes   ___ seldom   ___ never

10. Student shows confidence and self-assurance in his actions toward teachers and classmates.
___ always   ___ usually   ___ sometimes   ___ seldom   ___ never

Source: Adapted from *The antecedents of self-esteem,* by Stanley Coopersmith. Freeman, 1967. Reprinted with permission of J.T. Edmondson.

Behavior Rating Scales

There are many commercially produced rating scales that a teacher may use to observe student behavior.

1. *Behavior Problem Checklist*
   Available through:
   Dr. Herbert Quay
   Department of Applied Social Sciences
   University of Miami
   Coral Gables, Florida 33124
   This scale has been the most widely researched scale in literature. The research conducted in its development and subsequent use suggests that it serves as a reliable tool to differentiate among the learning disabled, emotionally disturbed and normal student populations.

2. Devereaux Adolescent Behavior Rating Scale
   Available through:
   Devereaux Foundation Press
   Devon, Pennsylvania 19333
   Devised by G. Spivack and M. Swift, it may be used with students aged 13-18.

3. Jesness Behavior Checklist
   Available through:
   Consulting Psychologist Press, Inc.
   577 College Avenue
   Palo Alto, California 94306
   Devised by C.F. Jesness, it is appropriate for use with grades 7-12. There are two forms of this instrument: an Observer Form, for ratings by teachers, counselors, etc.; and a Self-Appraisal Form for self-evaluations. It is excellent for evaluating behavioral change in school and for comparisons between self and observer ratings.

4. Burks' Behavior Rating Scales
   Available through:
   Arden Press
   8331 Alvarado Drive
   Huntington Beach, California 92646
   Devised by H.F. Burks, it is intended for use through grade 8. The ratings are scaled on a profile clustering each category into: not significant, significant, and very significant. This instrument has demonstrated an ability to show changes in a student's behavior patterns over a period of time and has provided a source of material to school personnel for conferences with parents.

Student Role Questionnaire

A learning disabled student is frequently unaware of his study habits and how inefficient study skills often contribute to his learning problems.

It is helpful for the teacher to provide a guide that the student may use in analyzing his role as a student. (See Exhibit 1-3.)

Exhibit 1-3 Student Role Questionnaire

Please respond to each question asked so that we may work together in improving your learning ability.	Yes	No
Classroom Behavior		
1. Are you able to settle down easily?		
2. If seating is your choice, do you usually sit in the back of the room?		
3. Do you participate in class discussions?		
4. Do you ask questions?		
5. Do you attend to class lectures?		
Task Behavior		
6. Do you keep up with assigned readings?		
7. Do you take notes on homework assignments?		
8. Do you read all the material in an assignment (i.e., charts, graphs, etc.)?		
9. Do you feel adequately prepared most of the time?		
10. Do you find the vocabulary a problem in your ability to understand the material?		
Personal Behavior		
11. Do you feel "okay" about yourself as a student?		
12. Do you feel disorganized (unable to do well because you can't keep things together)?		
13. Do you feel that your grades reflect the amount of effort you have put into the course?		
14. Do you get angry, frustrated with school frequently?		
15. Do you feel comfortable in asking for help when you need it?		

The questionnaire in Exhibit 1-3 is an effective tool to use in discussing with the student ways that he might improve his learning capacity. The teacher may wish to share with the student that the differences between individuals in their capacity for success in work and study as determined by Maddox (1963, p. 11) are:

1. Intelligence and special abilities   50-60 percent
2. Industry, effort and effective study methods   30-40 percent
3. Chance and environmental factors   10-15 percent

The teacher's objective in this activity is to enable the student to see that his behavior can affect learning—both positively and negatively—and that personal effort is a significant factor in academic success.

STUDENT LEARNING STYLES: HOW TO TEACH EFFECTIVELY TO EACH STUDENT

Each type of student requires a special teaching approach.

The Inflexible/Inhibited Student

This student is characterized by a general unresponsiveness and aloofness. In addition, he has an underlying inability to adapt easily to changes in routine or structure. This student rigidly adheres to the rules of the setting, fearful of assertive or initiative behavior. Because of his preoccupation with structure, he frequently is not tuned into what is happening in his surroundings. This student frequently responds with answers unrelated to the questions asked. Often his nervousness causes him to misinterpret simple statements. These responses are adapted from Barkner (1971, p. 5).

Teacher Response

The teacher's primary task in providing instruction for the inflexible student is to reduce the ambiguity and complexity of educational tasks. This is best accomplished by presenting information in a concrete manner (i.e., with frequent examples) and by reducing alternatives. The teacher should try to maintain an easy routine that is still basically structured, which alleviates the pressures pushing the student to conform to a rigid system.

This student requires a supportive setting. Accepting him "where he's at," and providing structure to the student as he requires it, creates opportunities for him to express his knowledge.

The teacher should attempt to facilitate the student's self-monitoring of his performance. Requiring the student to support his statements with objective data helps make him aware of exactly what he is saying.

This student must be encouraged to attempt new experiences and activities. Role playing, simulation exercises, and frequent feedback on the appropriateness of his performance enhance the student's feelings of confidence and motivate him to explore the unknown. Successful experiences are the most effective means for encouraging the student to continue to venture into new situations.

The Antisocial Adolescent

This student's behavior is characterized by aloofness toward the teacher. His tendency is to direct disrespectful comments to adults and to place the onus for his educational problems on his teacher. This student frequently violates school rules, especially those that prohibit lying and stealing. The antisocial adolescent lacks tolerance for any task that offers him no inherent reinforcement. He often manifests this lack of tolerance through temper tantrums; thus, much teacher attention is needed to keep him at a task. The following responses are adapted from Barkner (1971, p. 5).

Teacher Response

Avoid punishment! Punishment often creates feelings of hostility in the student, while being of scant effectiveness in reducing the frequency or intensity of the deviant behavior. It is important, however, that the teacher give immediate and consistent responses to the student's inappropriate behavior. The teacher should respond to inappropriate behavior by suggesting the approved or appropriate behavior expected from the student.

Immediate feedback to the antisocial student about the social consequences of his behavior should be delivered in a depersonalized manner. The student should be helped to see that society dictates behavioral standards. This suggests that consequences for deviancy be clearly defined for the students in a careful manner. If the student perceives the feedback as moralizing or preaching, he will probably "tune out" the teacher. If the student perceives the feedback as a personal attack, the teacher can expect increased hostility.

The student should be encouraged to think through the cause-and-effect relationships of his behavior and others' responses to it. The teacher should try to enable the student to think before he behaves.

A teacher should require the antisocial adolescent to support his generalizations. When the student gets into the "blame game" (e.g., blaming the teacher or suggesting that others are out to "get" him), he must be made to see that these statements are gross generalizations without (most often) any basis.

The Overachiever/Anxious Student

This is the student whose self-esteem is almost totally a function of others' opinions. His prime concern is to please others, attempting to gain his teacher's approval by producing more work than his classmates. He is competitive, and jealous of peers. Outward nervousness during tests is one behavioral indicator of the student's extreme fear of failure. His behavior with teachers is usually friendly.

Teacher Response

Reduce the importance of grades. Use them as only one of many measures of the student's achievement or progress.

Permit the student to evaluate his performance against objective, definitive standards.

Create a climate that is tolerant of the student's mistakes. This will decrease the pressure the student imposes on himself to maintain a record of perfect behavior.

Construct situations in which the student is required to think. This forces him to direct his energies to the cognitive domain, rather than react on an emotional level.

Innovative/Intuitive Student

This student is characterized by creative thinking and an openness to new ideas. This student is commonly able to describe things in an interesting manner, is likely to know class material when called upon, and is persistent in problem solving.

Teacher Response

Flexibility is the key to success with this student. Allow the student alternatives to paper and pencil tasks to express his knowledge.

Opportunities for creative expression and open-ended activity should be provided this student within the classroom structure.

Relate the student's creative accomplishments (products) to his reality and experiences. This approach serves as a vehicle for the teacher to slowly build structure and rules into the student's creative expression.

SUMMARY

With the LD adolescent whose problems in school are magnified by adolescence itself, behaviors rarely fall neatly into a specific profile. In addition to developing an overall characterization of a student's behavior, the teacher must focus attention on discrete problems that preclude the student's achieving his potential.

REFERENCES

Barkner, J.M. *Learning styles*. Dayton, Ohio: Institute for Development of Educational Activities, 1971.

Clements, S.D. *Minimal brain dysfunction in children*. (NINDB Monograph No. 3, U.S. Public Health Service Publication No. 1415). Washington, D.C.: U.S. Government Printing Office, 1966.

Coopersmith, S. *The antecedents of self-esteem*. San Francisco: Freeman, 1967.

Havinghurst, R.J. (Ed.). *Developmental tasks and education* (3rd ed.) New York: David McKay Publishing Co., 1972.

Kuhlen, R.G. *The psychology of adolescent development*. New York: Harper, 1952.

Maddox, H. *How to study*. Greenwich, Conn.: Fawcett Publishing Co., 1963.

National Advisory Committee on Handicapped Children. *Special Education for Handicapped Children*. First annual report. Washington, D.C.: U.S. Department of Health, Education and Welfare, 1968.

Watson, G. What do we know about learning? *National Education Association Journal*. Washington, D.C., 1963.

ANNOTATED SUGGESTED READINGS

Learning Style
Rita Dunn and Kenneth Dunn, *Educator's Self-Teaching Guide to Individualizing Instructional Programs,* West Nyack, New York: Parker Publishing Company (1975): Chapter 3. Describes, and provides the research basis for, the 18 elements of learning style; includes the Learning Style Questionnaire and a Profile Form for recording individual data.
Administrator's Guide to New Programs for Faculty Management and Evaluation, West Nyack, New York: Parker Publishing Company (1977): Chapters 3, 5, and 6. Describes how to appraise faculty teaching styles and then expand them to respond to varied student learning styles.
How to Raise Independent and Professionally Successful Daughters, Englewood Cliffs, New Jersey: Prentice-Hall, Inc. (1977): Chapter 4. Explains how to test for a child's learning style (Learning Style Questionnaire included) and how to match learning style characteristics and instructional programs; provides a sample case study designed to help determine proper school placement on the basis of learning style differences.
Teaching Students Through Their Individual Learning Styles: A Practical Approach, Reston, Virginia: Reston Publishing Company (1978). Provides the research basis for learning style; describes the Learning Style Inventory (a computer-based program for identifying individual and group clustered learning style differences); describes, on a step-by-step basis, how to design and match resources, methods, and programs to varied learning style elements; and includes a research supplement on the relationships between learning style characteristics and I.Q., reading achievement, math achievement, and self-concept.

SUGGESTED READINGS

Bateman, G. An educator's view of a diagnostic approach to learning disorders. In J. Hellmuth (Ed.), *Learning Disorders*. Seattle: Special Child Publications, 1965.

Bryant, N.D., & McLoughlin, J.A. Subject variables: Definition, incidence, characteristics, and correlates. In N.D. Bryant and C.E. Kass (Eds.), *Final Report; Leadership Training Institute in Learning Disabilities*, (Vol. 1). Tucson: University of Arizona Department of Special Education, 1972.

Griffin, M. How does he feel? In E. Schloss (Ed.). *The adolescent with learning disabilities*. San Rafael, Calif.: Academic Therapy Publications, 1971.

Hammill, D.D. Defining "learning disabilities" for pragmatic purposes. *Academic Therapy*, 1976, *12*, 26-37.

Kirk, S.A. *Educating exceptional children* (2nd ed.). Boston: Houghton Mifflin Co., 1972.

Kirk. S.A., & Bateman, B. Diagnosis and remediation of learning disabilities. *Exceptional Children*, 1962, *29*, 73-78.

Myklebust, H.R. Psychoneurological learning disorders in children. In S.A. Kirk and W. Becker (Eds.) *Conference on Children with Minimal Brain Impairment*. Urbana: University of Illinois Press, 1963.

Reynolds, M.C., & Balow, B. Categories and variables in special education. *Educational Children*, 1972, *38*, 357-366.

Strother, C., Hagin, R., Griffin, M., & Rogan, L. *The educator's enigma: The adolescent with learning disabilities*. San Rafael, Calif.: Academic Therapy Publications, 1971.

Telford, C., & Sawrey, J. *Educational psychology: Psychological foundations of education*. Boston: Allyn and Bacon, Inc., 1968.

Weiderholt, J.L. Historical perspectives on the education of the learning disabled. In L. Mann and D.A. Sabatino (Eds.). *The second review of special education*. Philadelphia: JSE Press, 1974.

Wiederholt, J.L. *A Report on Secondary School Programs for the Learning Disabled*. Final Report. (Project No. H12-7145B, Grant No. OEG-0-714425). Washington, D.C.: Bureau of Education for the Handicapped, 1975.

Ysseldyke, J.E. Diagnostic-prescriptive teaching: The search for aptitude-treatment interactions. In L. Mann and D.A. Sabatino (Eds.). *The First Review of Special Education* (Vol. I). Philadelphia: JSE Press, 1973.

Chapter 2

Teaching the Adolescent How to Learn

2

TEACHING THE ADOLESCENT HOW TO STUDY

The LD adolescent profits when tasks are structured, broken down into discrete steps and presented to him in a sequenced manner.

Expanding upon Robinson (1961), the following guidelines are suggested as an approach to enhance the study effectiveness of the LD student.

1. The student should first obtain an overview of the assignment. He should begin by writing exactly the assignment task the teacher has given—is he to read? to answer questions? to outline?
2. With a definitive purpose in mind, the student can more efficiently address the task. He should write what he hopes to gain as a result of his effort so that he has a clear and concrete goal to serve as a guide.
3. The student should use the aids provided through the structure of the text. Chapter titles, subheadings, summaries are valuable to the student in taking notes of "important" information. Further they provide "cues" to the student of the information that *is* important.
4. The next step is actually outlining or noting information in organized manner. The teacher can assist here by asking the student to write *only* the information he feels is the most important and using this as a basis for comparing with the teacher's notes. (A tendency of many students is to copy verbatim or to take excessive notes without really assimilating the information.)
5. The student should attempt to summarize the material in the assignment (with the goal he has established for the reading in mind). He should ask himself the following questions: have I the necessary information to meet the goal? am I able to discuss the main points in my own words? what does this material really mean?

Teaching the Student to be a Better Test-Taker

After the LD student has been given direct instruction in more effective learning approaches, he should be taught how to more effectively demonstrate what he has learned.

One approach is to present suggestions to the student in a Learning Activity Packet, as in Exhibit 2-1. This approach enables him to study independently as needed on an individualized basis. Maddox (1963, pp. 115-117) offers additional suggestions.

TEACHER-MADE TESTS

For the purpose of measuring student progress, the teacher has several options. In selecting a measuring instrument, the objectives should be clear. The purpose of evaluation is to determine:

1. the beginning level of instruction;
2. the pacing of instruction and feedback to the learner; and
3. final achievement level.

Numbers "1" and "2" above are called "formative" evaluation, since their major objective is to help the student by providing feedback on his errors, his rate of progress, and his level of achievement relative to the acceptable level of competence.

The third finding—the final achievement level—is called "summative" evaluation. Each test form has its own strengths and weaknesses, as follows (Green, 1970, pp. 6-7):

Oral Test

Strengths	*Weaknesses*
1. Permits extensive measurement	1. Is time-consuming
2. Is useful as an instructional device	2. Results in poor pupil performance due to lack of practice
3. Permits teacher to provide student with cue to elicit desired responses	3. Provides limited sample unless pupils are tested individually
4. Improves test rapport for pupils who fear written exams	4. Is frequently poorly planned
5. Is particularly useful in such fields as foreign language and speech	5. Provides no written record

Exhibit 2-1 Learning Activity Packet

How to be a Better Test-Taker

To the Student:

If you have ever studied for a test only to find your efforts didn't pay off in a good grade because you didn't study efficiently, this packet can help. Follow the suggestions in the order presented. Read each item carefully. Review wherever you feel necessary.

Begin!

1. When taking a test, don't panic! Be prepared by having a pencil (with eraser), pen and paper.
2. Carefully examine the entire test before starting to answer any questions. It is very important that you understand what you are to do in response to the test. Knowing whether the teacher wants one word answers or discussion responses, for example, makes a difference in the correctness of your response.
3. After you have looked at the number of questions, the type of response required, estimate how much time you are going to devote to each question or area. Pay particular attention to the weight each question carries. An essay question worth 25 points out of 100 possible points must be given more time than two multiple-choice questions of 2 points each.
4. Answer first those questions you feel most confident of the answers.
5. When you are responding to an essay question, it is a good idea to write down the key ideas or main points in brief form. This will help you include everything you feel is of importance in your answer.
6. It is a good idea to try to answer all the questions in a test (unless you're told that you could be penalized for wrong answers). If you are really stumped on a question, go on to another. Sometimes another question will help you to remember the answer to the question you have been struggling with.
7. Write clearly. You are likely to lose points if the teacher has difficulty reading your writing.
8. Leave time to reread your paper before you hand it in. Pay attention to punctuation and spelling. Most importantly, ask yourself if you wrote what you intended.
9. In objective tests, don't waste time on questions that are confusing to you.
10. Once you have made a guess to a question you are unsure of, you should not change it: first guesses are usually best.

Objective Test

Strengths	*Weaknesses*
1. Gives an extensive test sample	1. Frequently neglects measurement of higher thought processes
2. Can be made highly reliable	2. May overemphasize rote learning
3. Can be graded objectively and quickly	3. Promotes poor study habits
4. Eliminates bluffing	4. Encourages guessing
5. Can be subjected to item analysis and further refinement	5. Is difficult to prepare
6. Can be adapted to several teaching objectives	6. Costs more than essay test to prepare and reproduce

Essay Test

Strengths	*Weaknesses*
1. Is applicable to measurement of writing and organizational ability	1. Gives a limited test sample
2. Is easy to construct	2. Is difficult to grade
3. Promotes proper type of study	3. Favors the verbally inclined student
4. Is adaptable to several subject fields	4. Encourages bluffing

Performance Test

Strengths	*Weaknesses*
1. Stresses application of knowledge	1. Is not applicable to many fields of learning
2. Can be used as a learning device	2. Is difficult to construct
3. May give a truer achievement picture for the verbally handicapped	3. Is often difficult to grade
4. Measures some skills and abstract abilities not measured by other conventional forms	4. Is often time-consuming

Source: Reprinted from *Introduction to Measurement and Evaluation* by John A. Green. Table 1 "Movement, Persons, and Events Important in the Development of Measurement and Evaluation." (pp. 16-17). Copyright © 1970 by Harper & Row Publishers, Inc. Reprinted by permission of the publisher.

TEST SELECTION

When a teacher attempts to evaluate student progress, the "form" in which the measurement is to be taken is a critical factor in determining the test reliability. This is of particular significance with an LD student whose disability may be a negative influence on performance relative to certain types of tests. A delineation of the strengths and weaknesses of various tests as related to adolescence and learning disabilities follows.

Oral Test

Advantages	*Disadvantages*
1. Allows for extensive evaluation and greater individualization	1. Student with deficient verbal skills performs poorly
2. Permits an alternative mode for an LD student with a writing disability (poor motor coordination)	2. The student with poor memory performs less well due to lack of opportunity for practice and recall
3. Enables the teacher to provide "prompts" to elicit the student's response	3. Inhibited student may feel uncomfortable in "open (verbal) vs. "written" response
4. Teacher may easily individualize by varying the level of difficulty of the questions on the same material	4. The student is provided no written feedback
5. The test may be taped for later practice and review	5. There is no written record to share with parents or the student

Objective Test

Advantages	*Disadvantages*
1. The teacher may grade easily and objectively	1. There is only "one" right answer—little latitude is provided
2. The student with limited verbal expression may more easily, through "fill in the blanks" or "multiple choice" responses, demonstrate his knowledge	2. Student who may have grasped the concepts in the material but cannot easily recall details is penalized
3. Students cannot easily "bluff"	3. Students may respond correctly through rote learning

Objective Test (continued)

Advantages	*Disadvantages*
4. Students who write poorly (motor coordination) are not penalized	4. Frequently only specific information is requested and higher level processing is sacrificed
5. Teachers may compare responses across the class	5. Students may inadvertently be encouraged to guess

Essay Test

Advantages	*Disadvantages*
1. Allows for individual expression	1. Limits the sample of areas to be measured
2. Promotes higher level processing	2. Favors the student with refined verbal expressive skills
3. The teacher may easily construct the test	3. It is difficult to grade with objectivity

Performance Test

Advantages	*Disadvantages*
1. Students who have verbal expressive difficulties have an option	1. Is limited in application
2. Does not easily allow for individualization	2. Favors the well coordinated student

Basic Rules of Test Making

Given that each test form has both advantages and disadvantages, it is essential that the individual responsible for test construction be conversant with the rules of test making.

Be sure to have the purpose of the test clearly in mind. To what extent are you trying to measure how well your students have learned a particular unit of study? To what extent do you hope to rank your students accurately according to their abilities? How highly diagnostic of the strengths and weaknesses of individual pupils do you want your test to be?

Make a careful plan for the test questions. Unless your test covers a very limited unit of work, the plans should be written, since most plans are not so simple that they can be kept firmly in mind. Furthermore, you are better able to recognize a test's strengths and weaknesses when you examine a *written* plan.

If your test is mainly diagnostic in a basic skill area, you should prepare at least ten questions—preferably more—for each subtest that you use. These subtests should yield separate scores on the various elements needed for mastery of the skill.

If you are trying to find out how well your class has mastered a particular unit of study, you should construct a test which parallels the work in class. Generally speaking, this test should not be too difficult. The commonly accepted passing score of seventy percent is appropriate for most classes.

When the major purpose of your test is to rank a selected group of students in order of their achievement, the questions should be on "critical" points of learning. These are the points that go beyond the superficial and obvious. They are "critical" in the sense that they are prerequisites for truly high-level achievement. Questions on "critical" points often require that the student understand implications, apply information, and recognize data. If, on the other hand, a test asks questions only on material that has been specifically taught in class and that must merely be remembered, scores are apt to bunch near the top of the range and, therefore, be of little help in determining an accurate ranking of achievement.

THE ACCOUNTABILITY ISSUE

The "Education for All Handicapped Act" (P.L. 94-142) will continue to have a significant impact on school systems, which are now required to provide appropriate programs for their special-education students. Accountability for student progress is a primary focus of the Act. This means that those responsible for educating special-education students are required to develop an Individualized Education Program (IEP) for each such student, wherein the facets of the student's educational plan are clearly delineated. Each IEP must identify the student's present level of educational functioning, the special services he requires, the duration of those services, the time spent in the mainstream, and the personnel who are to deliver the services. A Planning and Placement Team (PPT)—comprised of a school administrator, teacher, PPT coordinator, and any other person deemed significant in the design of the plan—meets and develops the IEP for each student.

The student's needs are identified through the use of behavioral objectives. Also known as "educational objectives," "terminal tasks," and "learner-expected outcomes," behavioral objectives have become (by mandate, if not by choice) part of every educator's "tools of the trade." These objectives have assumed a significant role in education because they offer several benefits to all participants in the educational process.

Student Benefits

From the student's perspective, behavioral objectives offer the following benefits.

He can begin instruction at a level where he can enjoy success. For the student with a long history of academic failure, this is essential.

He knows exactly what he is expected to achieve. Clear goals assist the student by presenting him with an achievable end and a realistic path toward that end.

He has available a variety of learning alternatives based on his needs, abilities, interests, and learning styles.

He can progress at his own rate. The student's performance growth is measured against an objective standard—not against his peers.

He has the opportunity to monitor his own progress and evaluate his own output.

He has the opportunity to become a self-directed learner.

Teacher Benefits

The teacher who is responsible for a student's growth derives the following benefits from the use of behavioral objectives.

He can evaluate the effectiveness of the instructional process, and revise it if necessary.

He can evaluate his own performance in terms of the student's accomplishment.

He has a more effective means to report the student's progress to all concerned.

He can measure the student's performance before, during, and after a learning sequence.

He can provide the student with a range of learning alternatives matched to the objective and tailored to the individual student.

He can integrate a variety of media and methods related to what the student is to accomplish.

Parent Benefits

Parents now participate in the educational process more frequently, more pervasively, and more importantly than ever before. When the school communicates student performance to parents in behavioral terms, parents derive the following benefits.

They better understand the school's curriculum in general, and what their child is learning in particular.

They can assess how well the school is meeting their child's needs.

They can appreciate the resources that are needed for their child to receive the most appropriate program.

HOW TO EVALUATE STUDENT PERFORMANCE

There are two basic approaches to the measurement of a student's progress. "Formative" evaluation is undertaken through the use of tests and other evaluative procedures while the instructional unit or program is in progress. "Summative" evaluation occurs at the end of the instructional unit or program.

Both methods are significant in that they both produce feedback to the student. The teacher's focus should be to enable the student to perceive knowledge as new material for comprehending, analyzing, and evaluating questions of personal and social significance. This focus requires that the student be taught *how* to think, not simply *what* to think.

In considering specific learning tasks for a student, a teacher must recognize that the student's feelings and emotions cannot be separated from his capacity to learn and act thoughtfully in his environment. The "total child" is a composite of three distinct but inseparable components: the cognitive, affective, and psychomotor domains.

The Cognitive Domain

Testing for Specific Information

The most common test of student learning is to require recall of specific information.

Example: The Civil War began in the year _____.

The teacher should, however, teach discrete but related facts to the LD student—his ability to recall will improve because of the relatedness of the information. This means that the teacher must explore ways of testing for detail other than asking the student to regurgitate what he has memorized by rote.

Example: Arrange the following events in their proper positions and order along the time line:

          The Civil War   The Great Depression
          World War I   World War II

1810   1830   1850   1870   1890   1910   1930   1950   1970

Testing for Comprehension

Testing for comprehension involves ascertaining whether the student can interpret, analyze, and extrapolate from given information. Test questions should serve as a review for the student.

> *Example:* Read the following passage from a novel; then answer the questions which follow.

(Passage)

1. The novel from which the passage is taken is _____
_____.
2. The author is _____.
3. The themes which best represent the passage are:
    a. _____
    b. _____
    c. _____

The essay question is commonly used to measure the secondary-school student's level of comprehension. LD students are frequently penalized on essay questions because of deficient expressive ability. The mainstream teacher should not eliminate the use of the essay, as this has been demonstrated effective in broadening the LD student's cognitive development and style. However, the criteria by which the teacher evaluates the student's response must be clearly stated and defined.

An essay question that requires the LD student to apply knowledge he has acquired is helpful to him in that it allows him to draw on his average or above-average intelligence. The teacher's structuring of the task is essential to the student's success with the "essay." In this, consideration should be given to the student's expressive ability. Where this is a difficulty for the student, the teacher can provide an outline for the student to fill in or suggest a specific guide for him to follow.

An example of an essay question tailored to an LD student is offered:

> *Example:* Among modern nations, the United States has the highest rate of assault, rape, robbery, etc. According to the 1969 report of the National Commission on the Causes and Prevention of Violence, John Truslow Adams has written: "Lawlessness has been and is one of our most distinctive traits." From your knowledge of American history, what events can you cite to support Adams' belief. Consider the type of U.S. government and the values of Americans. (Tanner, 1972, p. 13)

The essay book report for the LD student should be structured. An example is offered below.

Book Report Model

Student Name _____ Date _____
Complete the following information from the book you read:
Title _____ Publisher _____
Author _____ Date of Publication _____
    1. If you liked the book, tell why (what interested you most).
    2. If there was anything you did not like about the book, tell what it was.
    3. If there were illustrations or pictures, how did they make things clear?
    4. Would you recommend the book to a friend? Why? or Why not?
    5. Would you read another book on a similar topic? Why? or Why not?

Testing for Comprehension in Science and Math

The teacher working with an LD student in technical subject areas must test for comprehension beyond literal recall. In technical areas, the student has traditionally memorized a formula, then plugged a given value into the formula, so as to calculate an unknown. However, if the student doesn't understand a formula, he is apt to make errors in calculation. Furthermore, such a student is unlikely to transfer the information to new situations. The teacher's responsibility with the LD student is to (a) be sure that he understands the statements represent lawful relationships, and (b) ensure that he can use a given formula in a variety of contexts.

    Example: The ancient Greeks denoted the value of *pi* (π) as approximately 3.1416. What *relationship* does π represent?

The Affective Domain

The affective domain consists of general and specific categories that encompass possible learning outcomes that might be expected from instruction. This domain includes those objectives that emphasize feeling and emotion and methods of adjustment.

At the bottom of the hierarchy of affective learning is the student's "awareness" of a phenomenon. "Attending" and "responding" are the next two levels. Next comes the student's responding to the phenomenon with feeling. The student then conceptualizes his behavior and feelings, organizing them into a structure. Finally, the student incorporates this structure into his life-style.

Teachers often refuse to test a student's affective level of performance, arguing that their job is to evaluate acquisition of objective information; that it is difficult to measure the student's feelings, intentions, etc.; and that this area is nebulous and, therefore, subject to many interpretations. I would suggest that these reservations be shelved, given the need to address the total child in the learning process. Tanner (1972) offers many specific suggestions for the use of objectives in classroom contexts.

It is possible and advantageous to evaluate the student's learning through a marriage of cognitive and affective questioning. Cognitive questioning is designed to reveal a student's level of intellectual functioning. It seeks to discern the student's ability to interpret information, apply information to new situations, analyze information into its basic elements, synthesize data and evaluate information. Affective questioning reveals a student's preference for and conceptualization of a value.

Example: Read the following from the cover story of a national news magazine, concerning a candidate for president.

(Story)

a. Underline every "charged" or "loaded" word and phrase in the preceding news story.
b. Assume that you are the reporter. Rewrite the item so that it is slanted to create a favorable impression of the candidate. You are free to use "charged" or "loaded" words and phrases, but do not go beyond the facts presented. (Tanner, 1972, p. 51)

One interesting and motivating method of applying the hierarchy of educational tests in the classroom is with a student group which allows for interaction in the learning process.

Procedure
1. *Selection of topic.* All students should be able to read the same book or see the same film or play. The teacher introduces several options for topics to the students.
2. *Identification of members.* Those students who agree to read the book or attend the movie or play are identified and comprise the members of a group as a function of the topic chosen.
3. *Gathering information.* Time is set aside for reading or viewing for the purpose of collecting data on the chosen topic.

4. *Group interaction*. The teacher structures the group through providing specific questions as a reference guide for their investigation and later analysis of the material.
   a. *Facts* The teacher asks the group, "What did the work say?" The facts are gathered. The story is retold. When sufficient facts are gathered, the teacher leads the group to part b.
   b. *Interpretation* The teacher asks the group, "What does the work mean?" Some of the major ideas are identified and discussed.
   c. *Evaluation* One idea is focused on. The teacher asks the group, "Do you agree or disagree with this idea?" This usually produces a lively discussion.
   d. *Application* The teacher asks, "Now that you've read (or seen) this work and discussed it, how will it affect you?" This opens the discussion to higher levels of interpretation than book reports or unstructured group discussion usually permits.

The Psychomotor Domain

This domain includes those objectives that emphasize motor skills, such as handwriting, typing, swimming and operating machinery. Although this domain includes some learning skills common to most subjects (such as speaking and writing) it receives major emphasis in commercial subjects: music, art, home economics.

Performance skills play a dominant role in the instructional objectives in these areas.

REFERENCES

Green, J.A. *Introduction to measurement and evaluation*. New York: Dodd, Mead, and Co., 1970.

Maddox, H. *How to study*. Greenwich, Conn.: Fawcett Publishing Co., 1963.

Tanner, D. *Using behavioral objectives in the classroom*. New York: Macmillan, 1972.

Robinson, F.P. *Effective study*. New York: Harper and Row, 1961.

ANNOTATED SUGGESTED READINGS

Ahmann, J.S. & Glock, M.D. *Evaluating pupil growth*. (3rd ed.). Boston: Allyn and Bacon, Inc., 1967. See chapters 9 and 10 for discussions of validity and reliability.

Block, J.H. Teachers, teaching and mastery learning. *Today's Education*. November/December, 1973, *63*(7), 30-36. This brief article argues persuasively for the mastery-learning viewpoint. It also discusses adaptation of the model to group instruction.

Clark, H., & Starr, I.S. *Secondary school teaching methods*. New York: Macmillan, 1959. There is an excellent discussion of marking and reporting to parents in Chapter 12, which is practical and easily understood.

DeShaw, B. *Developing competencies for individualizing instruction.* Columbus, Ohio: Merrill, 1973. Has a sample learning package that can be used as a model for individualizing instruction. Also includes suggestions for writing measurable objectives.

Green, J.A. *Introduction to measurement and evaluation.* New York: Dodd, Mead, & Co., 1970. Chapter 11 illustrates the use of the essay examination in assessing a pupil's critical thinking and problem solving.

Johnson, S.R. & Johnson, R.B. *Developing individualized instructional material.* Palo Alto, California: Westinghouse Learning Press, 1970. This is a programmed text that shows the reader how to construct an individualized, instructional evaluation.

Mager, R.F. & Pipe, P. *Analyzing performance problems.* Belmont, California: Fearon, 1970. This book proposes a system for analyzing performance problems. It is interestingly written and informative.

Marshall, J.C. & Hales, L.W. *Classroom test construction.* Reading, Mass.: Addison-Wesley, 1971. A brief but good discussion of marking and reporting is included on pp. 188-196.

Marshall, J.C. & Powers, J. Writing neatness, composition errors and essay grades. *Journal of Educational Measurement,* 1969, 6, 97-101. This article reviews a research study indicating a direct effect of handwriting on essay grades.

Noll, V.H. & Scannell, D.P. *Introduction to educational measurement.* Boston: Houghton-Mifflin, 1972. Chapter 7 includes discussion of both test planning and construction. The treatment is brief but practical.

Remmers, H.H., Gage, N.L. & Rummel, J.F. *A practical introduction to measurement and evaluation.* New York: Harper and Row, 1960. Chapter 9 gives some very practical suggestions for assigning course marks, including a method of weighing the various factors important in the marks.

Sanders, N.M. *Classroom questions: What kinds?* New York: Harper and Row, 1966. It relates questioning to Bloom's taxonomy.

Wood, D.A. *Test construction.* Columbus, Ohio: Merrill, 1960. Chapter 10 includes a brief discussion of the essay test and gives some suggestions for improving its use.

SUGGESTED READINGS

Bateman, B. Three approaches to diagnosis and educational planning for children with learning disabilities. *Academic Therapy Quarterly,* 1967, 3, 11-16.

Block, J.H. (Ed.). *Mastery learning: Theory and practice.* New York: Holt, Rinehart and Winston, 1971.

Bloom, B. (Ed.). *Taxonomy of educational objectives.* (Handbook I: Cognitive domain). New York: McKay, 1956.

Bloom, B., Hastings, J.T., & Madares, G.F. *Handbook on formative and summative education of student learning.* New York: McGraw Hill, 1971.

Carrin, A.A. & Sund, B. *Developing questioning techniques: A self-concept approach.* Columbus, Ohio: Merrill, 1971.

Dewey, J. *How we think.* Lexington, Mass.: D.C. Heath & Co., 1933.

Gerberich, J.R., Greene, H.A., & Jorgensen, A.W. *Measurement and evaluation in the modern school.* New York: McKay, 1962.

Hairow, A.J. *A taxonomy of the psychomotor domain.* New York: McKay, 1972.

Krathwohl, D.A., Bloom, B.S., & Masia, B.B. *Taxonomy of educational objectives* (Handbook II: Affective domain). New York: McKay, 1964.

Valett, R.E. *Programming learning disabilities.* Palo Alto, Calif.: Fearon Publishers, 1969.

Wilson, J.A. *Diagnosis of learning difficulties.* New York: McGraw Hill, Inc., 1971.

Ysseldyke, J.E. and Salvia, J. "Diagnostic-prescriptive teaching: Two models." *Exceptional Children,* 1974, *41*, 181-185.

Chapter 3

Mainstream Intervention Strategies to Remediate the Most Common Educational Problems of the LD Adolescent

3

The LD adolescent's educational problems relate both to his specific disability and to the secondary school's mainstream environment. In responding to the student's learning difficulties, both factors must be addressed.

This chapter outlines various behavioral attributes of LD adolescents and suggests specific strategies for a teacher to use in overcoming the learning difficulties created by those attributes. In addition Weiss and Weiss offer excellent suggestions in *A Survival Manual,* 1974.

LIMITED CONCENTRATION TO TASK

The LD adolescent is often unable to achieve academic success due to his inability to concentrate on a task for extended periods of time. This is a function of many factors: the student's lack of interest in the topic, his lack of organizational ability, previous failure experience with similar tasks, and his perceived nonrelevancy of the task.

Interventions

Break down tasks into small increments of learning that are then presented to the student in a paced, sequential manner. Ensure that the student has acquired one skill before you present the next skill in the hierarchy of learning tasks. Through this careful tailoring of the task, the student's potential to succeed is significantly increased. Furthermore, successful experiences enhance the student's attending behavior.

51

Contract with the student to establish agreed-upon learning goals. Setting clear objectives and behavioral expectations is an effective strategy for managing student progress. A contract may assume a number of forms, but should include: (a) an agreement on the amount of work the student is to accomplish, (b) the specific tasks the student will address within a given time period, and (c) student and teacher signatures sealing the contract. Exhibit 3-1 contains two sample contract forms.

Structure the assignment for the student and provide him frequent feedback about the quality and appropriateness of the work he has completed. With an assignment that is to be completed over a long period of time, the student's attention to the task is increased if the teacher establishes weekly checkpoints.

Strive to show the student the assignment's relevance to his own life. For example, relate math operations to personal finance, banking, consumerism, comparative shopping, and the like. This approach gives the student special incentive to acquire math skills. To cite but one more example, social studies concepts seem more relevant if you present them by using the classroom as a microcosm of society.

Consider a nontraditional grading system wherein reinforcement is provided for the student's appropriate responses. On a composition assignment, for example, the teacher would provide two grades—one for the composition's content (ideas), the other for grammatical structure and accuracy of form. This approach allows the language-disabled student to receive positive reinforcement for his ability to express ideas and knowledge, while remedying his specific language deficiencies.

Use a nontraditional directed-reading approach for assignments involving reading (social studies, science, etc.). Establish a purpose for reading; e.g., reading to acquire specific information, reading to answer specific questions, etc. Providing the student with a focus for his reading task will enhance his attention to it.

Tailor the assignment to realistic expectations (i.e., so that the student perceives it as attainable). Further progress will be noted if assignments are directed to areas of the student's interest. What interests the student may be easily determined with a student questionnaire. With an LD student—who often finds it difficult to respond to open-ended questions—it is preferable to assess his interests through a forced-choice response method. Instead of asking a question such as "What topic would you like to write a composition on?," it is preferable to say: "This assignment will be a composition. You may choose a topic on one of the following: A___ B___ C___ D___ (topic choices)"; or "You may present your report as an oral report, written report, or group presentation. Please indicate your preference."

Exhibit 3-1 Contracting: Sample Forms

SAMPLE CONTRACT FORM A

This week I agree to work on the following units:

1)

2)

3)

I will demonstrate the completion of the task by:

Student's signature _____

Teacher's signature _____

Date:_____

SAMPLE CONTRACT FORM B

Student Contract

Name _____Date: _____

Student objectives 1)_____

2)_____

3)_____

Student's signature _____

Completion date_____

Teacher's signature_____

NOTE: The teacher may wish to include an indication of the acceptable level of performance on the objectives (i.e., state the criterion for completion).

EXCESSIVE MOODINESS

Adolescence is usually characterized by vacillating emotions. It is the degree, duration, and intensity of the mood that may make it "deviant" or "excessive."

Interventions

It is important to avoid responding "in kind" to the student; e.g., responding with anger to an angry student. Teachers who violate this rule create a "win-lose" situation, wherein both parties must behave in a manner that will allow them to "save face." Wait through the peak of the emotion before responding, and be particularly wary of confronting a student in the presence of his peers.

Avoid preaching or moralizing in attempting to modify a student's emotional state. Presuming to know "what the adolescent is feeling" usually produces a negative response. Instead, use lead-in phrases such as "it seems to me that," "it appears that," and "I get the feeling that." This approach allows the student to agree or to "correct" the teacher.

Don't negate the adolescent's feelings. Your message should be that while you understand the anger, frustration, or other feeling, the student must seek an appropriate manner of expressing that feeling.

NEGATIVE SCHOOL ATTITUDE

Frequent failures in school and continuous academic frustration leave many LD adolescents with negative attitudes toward school. This attitude manifests itself as poor participation, general apathy, or resistance to educational activities.

Interventions

Provide activities that allow the student to experience "small successes," thereby enhancing his feelings of self-worth.

Use counseling and reality therapy to assist the "turned off" student to confront the real world.

Teach to a strong, personal interest of the student, incorporating units that present the student with information relevant to his concerns. Find one area in which the student can experience success, then capitalize on it!

Consider this student for vocational testing. Self-esteem is, to a degree, a situational phenomenon. The student who has experienced failure in school should be afforded an opportunity to "feel good about himself" in a noneducational arena.

"TEDIOUS" READING

The adolescent who experiences significant difficulty with reading often will not complete assignments. On tests which involve his having to read through long questions, he may receive a low test score—not because he can't provide the answers, but because he can't read the questions. The teacher plays a significant role in structuring the lesson to enable this student to achieve success. Kerber (1975) suggests 13 teacher tasks applicable to any reading lesson. Teacher-pupil interaction is required in each of the tasks which include the need for the teacher to be: adequately prepared, structured in the presentation of the lesson, enabling of the student's self-correction, skillful in questioning, able to observe and evaluate each student's progress, capable to individualize for each reader based on the observation, and finally sensitive of timing as to when to end the lesson.

These suggestions are relevant for any group of students and for the learning disabled. This type of structure is essential to academic success. Key factors, in addition, are: individualization, supplementary activities, and motivation.

Interventions

- Be cognizant of the form in which the student's performance is evaluated.

- De-emphasize timed tests. Provide the student with additional time for task completion, which will alleviate the pressure under which he is laboring.

- Provide instruction in the skills of skimming and phrasing to enable the student to speed up his reading rate through thought groupings.

- Highlight important information in reading assignments. This may be accomplished through teaching "the parts of the book," such as summaries and chapter headings.

POOR COMPREHENSION

The adolescent who has deficient comprehension ability often performs poorly on tests, as he does not fully understand the material being presented.

Interventions

Use an appropriate test to measure the student's reading comprehension. Suggested materials for the LD adolescent are:

- *Traxler High School Reading Test.* This test basically measures the rate of reading and level of comprehension for grades 10-12. Bobbs-Merrill Co., Inc., 1720 East 30th Street, Indianapolis, IN 46218.

- *California Reading Test.* This test is designed to measure vocabulary and comprehension. It is appropriate for junior-high grades 7-9; the advanced test, for grades 9-college.

- *Comprehension Tests of Basic Skills.* An achievement test series for evaluating comprehension and reading vocabulary. Level 4 is designed for use with grades 8-12. California Test Bureau (A division of McGraw-Hill, Inc.), 4655 Chase Avenue, Lincolnwood, IL 60646.

- *Cooperative English Tests.* Contains a section on comprehension. Four forms for grades 12-14; three for grades 9-12. Educational Testing Service, 20 Nassau Street, Princeton, NJ 08540.

- *Kelly-Greene Reading Comprehension Test.* Group test designed to test the listening comprehension of students in various subject areas; appropriate for grades 9-13. Harcourt Brace Jovanovich, Inc., 757 Third Avenue, New York, NY 10017.

- *Gates-MacGintie Reading Tests.* Speed, vocabulary, and comprehension are measured. It is available at all grade levels through grade 12. The tests are read by the students and subject to a time limit. It is appropriate for small- or large-group testing. Teachers College Press, Columbia University, 1234 Amsterdam Ave., New York, NY 10027.

Develop word-attack skills basic to the comprehension of any subject matter. Students should be taught an adequate sight vocabulary. Material appropriate to secondary vocabulary instruction includes:

- "A Basic Sight Vocabulary," by E.W. Dolch in *Elementary School Journal* 36 (February 1936): 456-60. This is the most widely used word list. According to Dolch, the 220 words on the list comprise 65 percent of the service words used in the reading material of the first three grades. This list also has significance beyond the 3rd-grade level, since the frequency of use drops only to about 60 percent through the intermediate grades.

- "Durrell Intermediate Word List," by Donald Durrell in *Improving Reading Instruction* (Harcourt, Brace and World, 757 Third Ave., New York, NY 10017, 1956), pp. 367-372. A list of words of 4th- 5th- 6th-grade difficulty. This list was derived from 56 reading, social studies, and natural science tests at the indicated levels.

- "A Literacy Vocabulary for Adults," by M.A. Metzel, *Adult Education*, Winter 1966, p. 68. A pragmatic list of 5,000 words gleaned from many sources—government publications and forms, employment forms, menus, signs, etc. This list could serve as a basic reading, thinking, and speaking vocabulary for use with adult Americans in need of functional reading instruction.

Increase the student's comprehension of the subject matter by building an experience base from which the student may approach the ideas. Activities that have proven effective toward this goal are informal discussion, direct experience, visual aids, dramatization, and field trips.

Develop working concepts and vocabulary with the student through group discussion, models and pictures, and demonstrations.

Stimulate the student's reading interest by providing a realistic purpose for reading. You may, for example:

- indicate the relationship of the assigned selection to the total unit of material being studied. Maintaining a student's interest is easier if the context is as clear as the specific unit.

- provide background information on the reading assigned.

- locate the geographical setting for the student. Establishing a purpose for reading serves to stimulate the student's thinking during the reading, and aids his concentration.

Supplement the reading material with individualized, culminating activities. You might, for example, ask the student to write an original story using the same theme as the assigned material. Also note that arts-and-crafts projects or displays offer an array of alternatives to the student who is less able to demonstrate his knowledge through more traditional, paper-and-pencil responses.

Supplementary High-Interest Activities for Reading Instruction

Student Dictionary. This is a variation on the experience approach to the teaching of reading. It is based on deriving reading material from the student's speaking vocabulary and life experience. The student is asked to write a word on a card, look in the dictionary for synonyms or antonyms, and then record the word's definition. The student is thus able to review and broaden his vocabulary in an easy and interesting manner.

Comic Strips. With students who have difficulty putting events in their proper sequence, consider using comic strips. In this activity, comic strips are cut into sections. The student is then asked to place the sections in their proper order along a time line. Variations of this activity include asking the student to think of different captions, attaching a time and place to the story, and providing a different sequence to the story by changing one of the characters.

Scrapbooks. In this activity, the student collects articles on a topic of interest. It is adaptable to any subject area, and lends itself to many permutations. You can, for example, ask students to compare differing points of view on a particular issue, or to compare different writing styles as they appear in newspapers or texts or magazine articles.

Word Games. It is often difficult for the language-disabled student to see commonalities in concepts. Thus, categorization is difficult for this student. To remedy this difficulty, the teacher chooses a category (e.g., cars, sports), and the student names as many words as he can which fit into the category.

Deficient Reading-Connected Skills

Comprehending material in secondary-level content areas requires adequate reading skills. The student must be able to:

- put in sequence, from memory, the events of a story he has read;
- outline from memory the main events of a story he has read silently;
- locate information in what is read;
- note inconsistencies in what is read; and
- move beyond literal recall through the use of imagery in working with words.

Developing Comprehension

Secondary-level material places special pressure on the LD student because of its concept density and difficult vocabulary. The teacher should include specific comprehension instruction. A suggested guide for a reading lesson is shown in Exhibit 3-2.

Exhibit 3-2 Suggested Guide for a Reading Lesson

1. *Discuss the title.* What does the student think it means, and what does he think it tells him about the story?

2. *Discuss the pictures.* Are the figures, places, or items depicted unfamiliar to the student? If so, they should be discussed. Ask the student what the pictures mean to him.

3. *Check vocabulary.* Be sure that the student can pronounce key words in the story. Does he know their meaning? If a word has more than one meaning, try to explain all meanings, and then ask how the word is used in the story. If, when reading, the student makes a mistake or cannot read a word, supply the correct word and keep a record of each error.

4. *Oral or silent reading.* Ask the student to read aloud or silently, whichever he prefers. When teaching him to read silently for independent reading, try to set a purpose and suggest that he read to himself to see if he can find the answer. Once the student has had an opportunity to preview the material through silent reading and has some familiarity with the vocabulary, the teacher may request him to read the passage aloud.

5. *Check comprehension.* With the reading materials closed, ask questions.
   a. What is the story about?
   b. Do you think the title was a good one?
   c. Is this story based on real life experiences? How do you know it is true? Why is it so?
   d. What do you think will happen next?

6. *Check for factual information.* Ask questions about specific details in the story—such as the age of one of its characters.

7. *Help to skim-read.* If the student cannot answer questions, have him look back in the story, find the answer, and read it aloud. If he has trouble, help him to find the answer.
   a. Ask whether he located the answer near the beginning, middle, or end of the story.
   b. Tell him which page the answer is on.
   c. Tell him which paragraph the answer is in.
   d. Give him clue words to help him find the answer.

8. *List of words missing.* For the next session, work out some little exercise or game where the student is required to fill in incomplete sentences or to answer questions using words from the story he has read.

Exhibit 3-2 continued

> a. Give me a word that rhymes with _____.
>   (Offer word that rhymes with missing word.)
> b. What is the opposite of _____?
> c. Give me a word that begins with _____.
>   (Name the initial sound.)
>
> 9. *Enrichment/overlearning activities.* To ensure that the student retains the basic concept from a reading selection, each lesson or session should include a variety of practice and enrichment activities related to the content of that selection. These might include teacher-made exercises or drills related to word analysis skills, field trips, guest lectures, or simulation and role-playing activities.
>
> *Source:* Adapted from David A. Sabatino and August J. Mauser, *Intervention Strategies for Specialized Secondary Education,* pp. 311-331. Copyright © 1978 by Allyn and Bacon, Inc., Boston. Reprinted with permission.

Guided Listening Procedure*

A technique which has proven successful in enhancing a student's long-term retention was developed by A.V. Manzo in 1975. It can be easily integrated into the classroom.

This technique is an adaptation of the guided reading procedure. Its objective is to increase the student's long-term recall, and should be used once every two or three weeks. The teacher presents a ten- or fifteen-minute speech—on tape or by lecture—and then takes the class through the following steps, adapted from Manzo (1975):

1. The teacher sets the major purpose: "Try to remember everything you hear."
2. The teacher lectures, reads, or plays a recorded selection. If the teacher is lecturing, he records the lecture.
3. The teacher reminds the students that they were asked to remember everything. The students then write on a blackboard everything they can remember. (Two students may perform this task.) During this stage, the teacher presents and writes everything the students are able to recall. The teacher makes no corrections and asks no questions.
4. The teacher reads aloud everything on the board and directs the students to look for incorrect or missing information.

---

*Reprinted with permission of Anthony V. Manzo and the International Reading Association.

5. The students listen again to the tape, record, or reading to correct wrong information and obtain missing information.
6. The information on the board is amended and added to, as needed.
7. The teacher asks the students which ideas on the board seem to be the main ideas, the most important ideas, the ones they think they should remember for a long time. The teacher marks these items.
8. Now that the students have mastered the literal level of the selections, the teacher raises any inferential questions he feels are vital to complete understanding.
9. The teacher erases the board and tests short-term memory with a test that is not dependent on reading or writing skills (e.g., oral true-false or multiple-choice items).
10. The teacher tests long-term memory with a similar test containing different items several weeks later.

Reading Programs that Work

What makes a reading program effective? The United States Office of Education has listed, in a catalogue called *Educational Programs that Work* (1977), a number of programs they have proven effective. In order for the program to have been listed, it must have been certified by a 22-member panel as having met six criteria:

1. Did a change occur?
2. Was the effect consistent enough and observed enough to be statistically significant?
3. Was the effect educationally significant?
4. Can the intervention be implemented in another location with a reasonable expectation of comparable impact?
5. How likely is it that the observed effects resulted from the intervention?
6. Is the presented evidence believable and interpretable?

In analyzing these programs, the elements they appear to have in common are:

• The program is individualized. Specific skills needs and differing learning patterns are accommodated. There is a heavy emphasis on direct instruction of decoding skills.

• The curriculum is structured with hierarchical sequencing stated in behavioral objectives.

- Varied reinforcement and frequent repetition strategies are pervasive in the program.

- Reading is interrelated with other basic skills.

- There is a cumulative, consistent and varied testing program.

- There is positive and immediate reinforcement of instruction.

- Varied approaches to teaching reading are used with an emphasis on diagnostic teaching.

- Varied strategies are used to involve parents.

Suggested Reading Programs for Use with the LD Adolescent

1. *Breakthrough.* A series of four books with an accompanying teacher's manual. It is useful for developing vocabulary and comprehension.
   Allyn & Bacon, 470 Atlantic Ave., Boston, MA 02210
2. *Maintaining Reading Efficiency.* Exercises in reading skills for grades 7-12.
   Audio Reading Progress Laboratory. A set of tapes, progress books, and teacher's guide for junior-high use.
   Developmental Reading Distributors, 1944 Sheridan, Laramie, WY 82070.
3. *New Horizons Through Reading and Literature.* A focus on comprehension skills and outlining for grades 7-9.
   Laidlow Co., Thatcher and Madison, River Forest, IL 60305.
4. *Reading Comprehension Through Effective Reading Programs.* A paperbook series of three study books, tests, time- and practice-logs. Learn, Inc., 21 East Eaclid Ave., Haddonfield, NJ 08033.
5. *Modern Reading Skill Text Series.* Three books on comprehension clues and tapes for grades 7-12. Charles E. Merrill Publishing Co., 1300 Alum Creek Drive, Columbus, OH 43216.

The Learning Activity Packet

The teacher of adolescents must be aware of different techniques and methods of teaching specific skills. With any approach, the teacher must consider the student's social and emotional facets. Of particular importance is the adolescent's focus on independence.

A Learning Activity Packet (LAP) provides for a self-directed plan of action. It allows for the incorporation of any type of material or subject matter.

There are four basic sections in any LAP:

1. The objectives indicate what the student is to learn. These are written for the individual student, and specifically indicate the final behavior expected of him; e.g., "After completing this LAP, you will be able to outline a story."
2. The pre-test facet evaluates the student's competence with the subject matter before he begins the LAP. The pre-test allows a teacher to pace his students on an individual basis. A student who scores 90 percent or better on a pre-test is eligible to move on to another LAP.
3. In the instructional phase, the teacher gives the student directions to guide him to the stated objective; e.g., "Read a short story," or "Listen to a tape." Each LAP must provide the student with options, as well as allowing him to practice the specific task and to apply his newly acquired knowledge.
4. In the post-test phase, the teacher evaluates the student's level of proficiency relative to the stated objective.

The LAP is an effective technique for providing direction and security to the student, while also allowing him a degree of independence. Exhibit 3-3 contains a sample LAP.

Structure

In addition to the LAP, the teacher can increase a student's comprehension and academic functioning through structuring the student's learning environment. The teacher may:

- *present short assignments.* Thus, the student with limited concentration, poor attention to task completion, and a short attention span can experience success.

- *control the degree of verbal directions.* LD students who have deficient auditory sequential memory (i.e., students who can't remember what they've heard in the correct order) must have directions broken down into short parts, with the teacher presenting one direction at a time.

- *alternate the nature of the activity.* Students who have difficulty controlling their activity level can experience success if they alternate sitting activity with activity of a different type (exercises, movement, etc.).

Exhibit 3-3 Sample LAP

This Learning Activity Packet will help you identify the theme of a short story.

A. Answer the following questions and complete the statements:
   1. The definition of a theme is _____.
   2. An example of a theme is _____.
   3. Listen to tape #21 and state the story's theme. _____
   _____.
   4. A "theme" and a "moral" are the same thing. True or False? _____
   5. State other words which are similar in meaning to "theme" and "moral."_____

B. When you have completed the pre-test, take the answer sheet from the file and correct your responses.

C. If you scored four out of five correct responses, you may move to the next LAP level on theme. If not, please follow the directions below. (Here the teacher might refer the student to a supplementary tape; practice sheets, etc.) Practice using the suggestions offered in this material to assist you in improving your ability to correctly identify themes.

D. Take the following post-test:
   1. Alternative terms for theme are _____.
   2. A story theme I find interesting is _____.
   3. Identify the theme of tape #23.
   4. Write a story outline using your stated theme.

   Note: When you have successfully completed this LAP, your ability to identify a story theme is 90 percent.

   Proceed to the next LAP.

- *maintain a consistent emotional climate.* The teacher should maintain a stable and consistent emotional climate in the classroom, so that the student feels secure.

- *maintain realistic performance expectations.* It is important to determine each student's productivity level. The teacher must consider both the quality and the quantity of a student's output. The teacher must strive to maintain a balance between the student's capacity to perform, his level of comfort in performing, and the teacher's own expectations.

THE SLOW-LEARNING LD STUDENT

This student requires detailed and simplified directions for all assignments. Concrete illustrations and short-range projections are necessary.

Interventions

Provide an accepting and encouraging relationship. Teacher attitudes significantly affect the performance of the slow learner.
Pace the presentation of material relative to student's ability.

- introduce only a few concepts at any one time.

- Frequently review material that has been presented. Repetition is a key factor in this student's ability to retain information.

- Present material in varied contexts to enhance the student's motivation to review the material.

- Simplify explanations, materials, and techniques.

Chart the student's progress on a daily basis. One of the most effective motivators is positive feedback to the student regarding his progress.

- Have the student keep a card file. Note words that he has learned to spell or read.

- Provide short-range goals with achievable objectives.

- Do not underestimate this student's capacity to learn.

THE EXPERIENTIALLY-DEPRIVED LD STUDENT

This student has not had varied experiences to supplement classroom activities, either because of an inaccurate estimation of his capacity to learn or because of a lack of appropriate community resources.

Interventions

Make every effort to obtain a reliable estimate of the student's potential to learn. This requires the use of both informal tests and traditional measures.

Provide the student with direct instruction in "learning how to learn."

Teach reading as a life-related process. Obvious relevance of the material enhances the student's interest and attention.

Vary the approaches used to present reading material. Consider a modality approach (visual, auditory, multisensory).

Provide the student with a learning environment in which there is an atmosphere of trust. The use of programmed material allows the student to self-pace his learning, while permitting him to self-correct his responses.

Converse frequently with the student. Foster language development through role playing and dramatic representation.

Assist the student with long-term information retrieval in the following ways (Gagne, Bolles, and Golanter, 1959):

- Use active self-testing or recitation.

- Use groupings of information together with rhythm (e.g., the multiplication table and alphabet, taught in a sing-song fashion).

- Direct the student's attention to the meaning of the words or material, and use associations to trigger recall.

- Use reinforcement to create in the student a strong intention to learn.

THE SLOW READER

Many LD students have difficulty keeping up with their peers because they read slowly. Carefully diagnose the nature of the student's difficulties in subject areas as they relate to reading. If a teacher knows that a student's problems emanate from an inadequate vocabulary, an inability to vary his reading rate to suit the nature of the material, or simply a habit of slow reading, that knowledge should have a direct and significant effect on how the teacher presents material to that student.

If the student's reading speed for easy material is less than 200 words per minute, the following suggestions are offered as interventions.

Interventions

If the student's slow reading is due to subvocalizing (whispering to himself), require him to read rapidly enough to make such lip movements impossible.

Structure a daily session of systematic practice to improve a student's reading rate. Begin with 15-20 minutes per day, extending this for at least 3-4 weeks. Begin by using fairly simple, brief reading selections, such as newspaper and magazine articles.

Instruct the student to read each article as quickly as he can without sacrificing comprehension. Record the amount of time he requires to read each selection. Estimate the number of words in the article by multiplying the number of lines by the average number of words per line. Divide this figure by the number of minutes spent reading the selection to obtain the student's reading rate in words per minute.

Additional interventions are suggested by Deschant in *Diagnosis Remediation of Reading Disability* (1968).

Maintain a chart or graph of the student's reading rate. This provides clear daily feedback to the student as to his progress. With consistent practice over a reasonable period of time, the slow-reading adolescent should be able to increase his reading by at least 50 percent for easy material.

THE POOR SPELLER

Spelling instruction should be integrated in the total language-arts curriculum: good spelling is a *tool* to be used in communicating, not an end in itself.

Interventions

Have each student keep a notebook containing words he has misspelled in compositions or other written work. Alternatively, have the student count the spelling errors in the first hundred words of each composition.

Allow time for the student to write compositions on issues or topics which are of personal interest. The vocabulary he generates on his own becomes the basis for improving his spelling.

Suggest that the student keep a graph of his progress. Since the student can see his progress, his motivation often increases.

Establish realistic performance goals. This is an important step in maintaining the student's interest and attention to task. Have the student build a card file of words that he has mastered, thus providing reinforcement for progress and permitting easy review and practice of spelling words.

REFERENCES

Educational Programs that Work, Volume 4., Washington, D.C.: U.S. Department of Health, Education and Welfare, Office of Education, Winter, 1977.

Gagne, R.M., Bolles, & Golanter (Eds.). Automatic teaching. New York: Wiley Publishing Company, 1959.

Kerber, J.E. *The tasks of teaching reading.* Worthington, Ohio: Charles A. Jones Publishing Company, 1975.

Manzo, A.V. *Journal of Reading,* 1975, *1,* 287-291.

Sabatino, D.A. & Mauser, A.J. *Intervention strategies for specialized secondary education.* Boston: Allyn and Bacon, Inc., 1978.

Weiss, H., & Weiss, M. *A survival manual: Case studies and suggestions for the learning disabled teenager.* Great Barrington, Mass.: Treehouse Associates, 1974.

SUGGESTED READINGS

Christ, F.L. *Studying a textbook.* Chicago: Science Research Associates, 1966.

Deighton, L.C. *Vocabulary development in the classroom.* New York: Teachers College Press, 1959.

Deschant, E. *Diagnosis and remediation of reading disability.* New York: Parker Publishing Co., Inc., 1968.

Gagne, R.M., Bolles, & Golanter (Eds.). A review of the factors in learning efficiency in *Automatic Teaching.* New York: Wiley Publishing Company, 1959.

Gordon, A.K. *Games for growth.* Palo Alto, Calif.: Science Associates, College Division, 1970.

Hoover, K.H. *The professional teacher's handbook: A guide for improving instruction in today's secondary schools.* Boston: Allyn and Bacon, Inc., 1973.

Jackson, S.J., "The quest for reading programs that work," *Educational Leadership,* December 1978.

Joyce, B. & Weil, M. *Models of teaching.* Englewood Cliffs, N.J.: Prentice Hall, 1972.

Kim, E.C. and Kellough, R.D. *A resource guide for secondary school teaching: Planning for competence.* New York: Macmillan, 1974.

Manzo, A.V. Guided Reading Procedure. *Journal of Reading,* 1975, *1,* 287-291.

Sabatino, D.A. and Mauser, A.J. *Intervention strategies for specialized secondary education.* Boston: Allyn and Bacon, Inc., 1978.

Tallmadge, K.G. *Ideabook.* Washington, D.C.: U.S. Department of Health, Education and Welfare, October 1977.

How to Succeed in the Content Areas

4

In the field of education, the term "content areas" usually refers to particular, specialized fields, such as science, mathematics, literature, social studies, and home economics.

In order for the mainstreamed LD adolescent to survive in these areas, he must have achieved at least a minimal proficiency in reading. The vocabulary of secondary-level material is difficult, new terms are introduced rapidly, few explanations are provided, and great retention is demanded. At the same time, fewer supportive programs are provided to students at this level.

The skills necessary for successful content work generally fall within the realm of study skills. Students are required to (1) locate information through the use of tables of contents and indexes; (2) interpret maps, pictures, graphs, and charts; and (3) organize materials with outlines and summaries.

Most LD adolescents have long histories of educational failure, owing to inappropriate instruction—instruction that is not carefully structured, paced, and sequenced. The potential for continued failure is inherent in the manner in which secondary-level content materials are written: numerous facts and ideas are packed into a relatively small space ("concept density"), while there are few organizational clues in the form of headings, subheadings, and boldface type to highlight *important* facts and ideas. The specificity and unfamiliarity of secondary-level vocabulary constitute major handicaps for LD students in the content areas. It is relatively easy to see that comprehension and interpretation suffer as a result.

This chapter provides the teacher an arsenal of strategies with which to battle the built-in obstacles that impede the progress of the mainstreamed LD adolescent.

One of the most basic tools a teacher can use to assure the student's success is an appropriate and effective method for presenting content.

71

TASK ANALYSIS: A FOOLPROOF METHOD FOR PRESENTING CONTENT

"Task analysis" is a proven technique for increasing the effectiveness of instruction. There are two basic analysis approaches: a "behavioral" approach and a "modality" approach.

Behavioral Task Analysis

The subject matter to be taught is broken down into its basic elements. The skills and concepts are then sequenced and presented in a carefully prescribed format.

Assume, for example, that the teacher has asked the LD student to read and outline five pages of a textbook. In reviewing the student's outline, the teacher notes that the student did not identify the main idea of the passage; instead, he outlined only the supportive ideas and details. The teacher might respond by "tailoring" the assignment, as follows:

Initially ask the student only for the main idea in each paragraph. Assist him by having him respond to the following questions.
a. What is the subject of this paragraph?
b. What leads you to believe that the idea you've said is the main idea of this paragraph is in fact the main idea?
c. What is the relationship between (1) the main idea of this paragraph, and (2) the previous paragraphs?

The teacher's objective here is to help the student see the continuity of the material (the part-to-whole relationships). This technique integrates the material's specific details in a comprehensive unit, thereby aiding the LD student who has inadequate associative ability. The teacher should extend this concept by relating (1) each night's homework assignment to the previous night's, and (2) specific objectives to broad goals. With practice, the student increases his ability to focus his attention and to differentiate between salient and trivial information. Consistent, long-term use of this approach eventually helps the student to *automatically* focus his attention appropriately.

Modality Task Analysis

The second approach to a task analysis employs sensory modalities. This approach is predicated on the premise that most individuals have a preferred sensory channel for learning—meaning that some people are better auditory learners, some are better visual learners, and some learn best when these senses are combined (multisensory learners).

This approach is of particular significance with the LD student, because inherent in the LD label is a presumed deficiency in processing via one of the senses. For example, the student who has an auditory sequential memory problem (i.e., one who can't remember the order of what has been said) is at a severe disadvantage in most secondary-level classrooms, where the lecture is the principal method of instruction.

The modality approach looks at (1) the manner in which material is presented (i.e., whether it is auditory, visual, or a combination of the two), and (2) the mode of response which is required of the student.

Assume, for example, that the teacher writes notes on the blackboard, which the student is to copy into his notebook. The presentation is visual; the required response is motor (writing). In checking the student's notebook, the teacher observes that the notes are poorly written, contain frequent markovers, and are incomplete. In analyzing the student's performance, the teacher notes an awkward pencil grasp, poor movements in the formation of letters, and laborious writing effort. The teacher may thus determine that poor fine-motor skills (writing ability) and/or poor far-point copying ability (from blackboard to paper) are factors barring the student's success. It is important, however, that the teacher clearly understand the objective of the lesson. If the teacher's aim, for example, is that the student learn the ideas within the assignment—*not* that the student be competent in copying—the assignment may be modified to highlight this aim. A partial outline—wherein the student is responsible only for filling in the missing information—allows the student to focus his attention on the passage's ideas, and not (of necessity) on the writing task itself.

Task Analysis in Five Easy Steps

Whichever task analysis approach the teacher elects to use, he must follow a basic sequence of five steps:

1. *Review* the content to be taught. Consider the teaching materials available, the specific skills of the student, and the objectives of the lesson. Select concepts to be emphasized and details to be learned. These should be listed for later use in constructing study guides and test questions.
2. *Survey* the material for words and phrases that the student may find difficult to recognize or understand. Decide which words will be pretaught, which ones will be simply pointed out and pronounced, and which ones are unimportant enough to be ignored. Plan the methods to be used in teaching the selected words. Limit the number to no more than five in any lesson.

3. *Identify* the skills and processes the student needs to complete the learning task successfully.
4. *Plan* the lesson and study guide, considering the different levels of comprehension at which students function within any one class. For the student who is functioning on a literal level, for example, the teacher would want to list questions, providing the student with page, column, and/or paragraph numbers to guide him to correct answers. Those students who are operating at an interpretive level can answer conceptual and critical questions (e.g., "What does it all mean?"). Those functioning at the most advanced level can apply information and generalize, and questions at this level should force the synthesizing of facts into generalizations. These students may be asked to use other references, past experiences, etc., to find answers to the stated questions.
5. *Gather* the needed information and *prepare* the materials for presentation.

HOW TO DETERMINE READABILITY

It is important that the materials a teacher uses with students on the secondary level be reviewed to assess their appropriateness for use with the student group for which they are intended. The "readability" of textbooks and materials is directly related to a student's ability to comprehend the concepts therein. Every mainstream teacher should master at least one method of measuring the reading difficulty of material designated for use with a secondary-level student group.

In most secondary-school systems, a curriculum committee selects the instructional materials to be used in content areas. In this selection process, many variables must be considered, one of which should be whether a text's readability is appropriate for the grade level for which it is being considered. The committee should determine, for example, whether a history text to be used with sophomores (grade 10) is written for comfortable reading by students at that level.

Measuring readability is a quick and simple task that can save both student and teacher countless hours of frustration in the long run.

The most prominent readability formulas all consider two factors:

1. *Word difficulty*. The greater the number of long or unusual words, the more difficult the selection is likely to be.
2. *Sentence length*. Longer and more complex sentences are strong indicators of more difficult selections.

A simple, fairly reliable formula to determine readability was developed by Fry (1963), a national expert in the area of reading, and is reproduced in Exhibit 4-1.

Exhibit 4-1 A Practical Readability Formula

1. *Select* three 100-word passages from near the beginning, middle, and end of the book or the material in question.

2. *Count* the total number of sentences in each 100-word passage. Estimate to the nearest tenth of a sentence. Average these three numbers by adding them together and dividing by three.

3. *Count* the total number of syllables in each 100-word sample. There is a syllable for each vowel sound, e.g., cat = 1; blackbird = 2; continental = 4.

4. *Do not* be deceived by word size (e.g., polio = 3; through = 1). Endings such as -y, -el, and -le usually make a syllable; ready = 2. Average the total number of syllables contained in the three samples of reading taken.

5. *Plot* on a graph the location of the two points to determine the grade level of the material.

6. *Choose* more passages per book if great variability in the student's reading performance is observed.

Your objective is to determine when faced with uneven reading performance whether this is a function of the student's reading response or a function of uneven readability of the book.

Source: Reprinted from *Teaching Faster Reading,* by Edward Fry, with permission of Cambridge University Press, © 1963.

COPING WITH TECHNICAL VOCABULARY

The adolescent with a reading disability must be given assistance with the technical vocabulary of secondary-level subjects.

There are a number of general guidelines which the mainstream teacher may easily integrate into his instruction, all of which are applicable to all language-disabled students.

- *Preview lessons before assigning them.* Specific attention should be given to vocabulary that the teacher anticipates will present students with problems of either recognition or comprehension.

- *Attempt to teach word parts.* Learning prefix and suffix meanings enables students to recognize unknown words to some degree.

- *Encourage students to keep vocabulary notebooks.* A student's ability to recall a word's spelling and meaning is reinforced by his writing it down.

- *Use audiovisual aids to clarify meanings.* Difficult vocabulary may be put on tape, followed by definitions. Cues that will aid the student in associative recall may also be provided.

- *Accompany vocabulary with appropriate synonyms and antonyms.* This builds the student's vocabulary beyond the specific lesson being taught.

For an example of how these guidelines can be incorporated in a lesson, see Exhibit 4-2.

Exhibit 4-2 A Lesson

Explain that the word "unsophisticated" means "not experienced with the ways of the world"; that the prefix "un" means "not"; that its synonyms include "naive," "ingenuous," and "artless"; that its antonyms include "sophisticated" and "worldly-wise"; that it is spelled u-n-s-o-p-h-i-s-t-i-c-a-t-e-d. If you use a tape recorder, the student can study the tape during a study hall, play it back for review, and learn the lesson at his own speed. The words may then be transcribed into the student's vocabulary notebook.

TEACHING STUDENTS TO ORGANIZE INFORMATION

The LD student's ability to remember concepts depends on his ability to organize information in a manner that will enable its retrieval. It is widely assumed that this ability develops automatically and is developmentally related. This assumption does *not* apply to the LD adolescent, who must be given specific instruction in organizing information. Failure to provide such instruction (as outlined below) significantly reduces the LD adolescent's capacity to recall concepts and facts.

- Teach categorization by having the student organize series of objects in categories. This allows him to see common attributes.

Man	Mars	Willow	Cod
Oak	Salmon	Pluto	Chimpanzee
Earth	Redwood	Ape	Tuna

Classify the words above by category:

Primates	*Planets*	*Trees*	*Fish*
(animals which have a backbone and walk on two legs)	(objects in the solar system)	(perennial plants)	(animals that live in water)

- Teach outlining. Allow the student to check his outline with a teacher's outline of the same material.

- Ask the student to select two or three main ideas in a series of paragraphs.

- Have the student group details about each of several main ideas.

- Have the student supply the details for an outline in which the main ideas have been supplied.

SOCIAL STUDIES

Map Skills

Social studies teachers face the task of teaching the mainstreamed LD adolescent to comprehend the symbolism that pervades maps and charts.

Begin the study of map skills with the student's own geographic location. Familiarity with neighboring cities and states will assist him in assimilating further information.

Planning a travel itinerary is an interesting way for the student to become familiar with map usage. Begin with a planned trip to an adjacent city.

Using an overhead projector, have the student draw maps containing specific information. He may be instructed to include capitals, major rivers, cities, etc. The amount of information in the map can thus be controlled.

Instruct the student to create his own imaginary "nation"—including maps of the "nation," names of "states," and pertinent descriptions. A brief report on the "nation"—including a description of natural resources, climate, etc.—may be required.

Control map elements when introducing the student to new map skills. Begin with a map that shows only the states, then add the capitals, then the rivers, and so on. Thus, the student can learn the variables gradually, rather than be overwhelmed by an abundance of new stimuli.

Town- and city-planning provides an interesting approach to the study of map skills on a local scale, and is conducive to a "project" format. For example, the student may use whatever materials are available to create a scale model of his ideal city.

Suggested Published Materials to Teach Map Skills

1. Scholastic Book Services: *Map Skill Book*. Series of eight workbook format tests.
2. Visual Materials Incorporated: *The United States in Maps*. D: Hols and transparencies.
3. Garrard Publishers: *Know your States:* Card games orientation to learning the location of states.
4. Hasenfeld Bros: Hasbrow: *United States Map Puzzle*.
5. Walch Publisher: *Map Activities for U.S. Geography Classes:* Series of visually simplified map dittos.
6. A.J. Nystrom & Co: *Learning to Use the Globe*. Contains directions for activities to be used in conjunction with globes.
7. Macmillan & Co: *Sullivan Programmed Geography*.

Directionality

Basic terminology essential to the comprehension of the directional aspects of maps should be specifically taught to the LD student.

Directional markers should initially be written directly on the map—north, south, east, west, longitude, and latitude.

Have the student draw a map of the school's interior. He can then direct other students to specific locations, using the appropriate directional terms.

Road maps may be used to plan trips. The student should be instructed to attend to the direction of the route (north-south or east-west).

Asking the student to plot the route to a favorite relative's house adds interest and motivation to the student's work.

Supplemental Materials to Teach Directionality

1. Houghton Mifflin - Windows on Our World Series, *The United States.*
2. American Book Co.: *Understanding Through Inquiry: The United States.* This is a teacher-directed text containing little written material, many pictorial representations.
3. Scholastic Book Services, *Map Skill Books.*
4. Visual Materials, Inc., *United States Geography.* This includes duplicating masters and transparencies.

Graphic Aids

When he uses graphics (maps, globes, charts, etc.) to supplement lectures and narrative assignments, the social studies teacher must recognize that the LD student must receive specific instruction.

Maps

The student should be instructed on the elements of a map and the information they offer him.

Suggest that the student study the map's title. In addition to providing information regarding geographic location, the title indicates the type of map being studied (topographic, climatic, demographic, etc.). The student must comprehend what he is studying, so that the interpretations he derives are related to a stable reference base.

Tell the student to study the map's legend and scale, and note the map's directions. The map's scale should be discussed to make the student aware of the geographic dimensions of the graphic. A comparison of various maps' legends will help the student put the information contained in the map into an accurate perspective.

Ask the student to relate the area under study to a larger area. The LD adolescent who has difficulty developing accurate part/whole relationships will benefit from the teacher's establishing the larger context into which the specific unit or area fits.

Time Concepts

One basic requirement of a social studies course is that the student comprehend the temporal relationships of historical events. This is difficult for many LD students who are deficient at sequencing or associating events.

Role playing of significant historical events helps to increase the student's awareness of those events.

Simulation games enable the student to develop perceptions within a historical context.

Time lines provide visual sequencing of events for the student.

Have the student create an imaginary family tree, then ask him to answer questions such as "During what war was your great-grandfather born?"; "When did your ancestors come to America?"; and "What did your ancestors find when they came to America?"

Ask the student to create time capsules from different periods of history. He can list items indicative of the period that would give people of the future an inkling into their lives.

Suggested Materials to Teach Time Concepts

1. Globe Publisher: *Social Studies for the Slow Learner.*
2. Pendulum Press: *Basic Illustrated History of America.* This material has comic book type illustrations which are correlated with tapes and filmstrips.
3. Imperial International Learning: *The Living History Book:* taped "news reports" of significant historical events.
4. Educational Insights: *American Revolution Simulation Games.*
5. Educational Insights: *Social Studies Strategies:* Teacher ideas for role playing.
6. Laidlow: *Social Studies Readers.* Story type presentation of historical events.
7. Fideler. *A Visual Teaching,* Social Studies Picture Program. Includes individual picture cards with questions and suggested activities.

Graphs

Social studies statistics are often organized in graphs, which allow a great deal of information to be presented in a compressed manner. The student must see that graphs offer relevant, essential information.

Make the student understand that graphs represent codified information. The teacher must help the student "decode" the graph.

Provide specific instruction on the meaning of vertical and horizontal lines within the graph.

Have the student identify the measuring scale utilized in the graph.

Ask the student to identify the conclusions that can be drawn from the graph.

Focus the student's attention on the graph's title, which indicates what the graph represents.

Information Location Skills

Mainstreamed LD students who have limited ability to concentrate and low tolerance for frustration often have little motivation to persevere with assigned tasks unless the teacher structures the learning situation so as to help them locate information. One way in which the teacher can provide this assistance is by teaching the student the structure (parts) of the subject textbook.

Teach the student to locate information by using the parts of a book. Indicate the purpose of the specific parts, such as:

- title page, author's name, publisher, publication date

- preface, introduction, foreword

- table of contents

- chapter headings and main headings

- glossary

Evaluating the Student's Locational Skills

Miller (1973, p. 215)* suggests that a teacher ask the LD student questions like those below to ascertain his competence in the use of a text's table of contents:

- How many parts does this book contain?

- On what page does Chapter 38 begin?

- How many chapters does this book contain?

- Is there a glossary in this book?

---

*From the book, *Diagnosis and Correction of Reading Difficulties in Secondary School Students*, by Wilma H. Miller. © 1973 by The Center for Applied Research in Education, Inc. Published by the Center for Applied Research in Education, Inc., West Nyack, New York 10994

- On what page does the chapter entitled "Radiation Biology" begin?
- How many sections does Part IV of this book contain?
- What is Chapter 19 of this book about?
- What section in this book is about insects?
- On what page does Chapter 13 begin?
- On what page does the index begin?

Teach the student to locate information in a dictionary.

- Review the alphabetical sequence.
- Teach the use and function of the "guide words."
- Teach the use of the pronunciation key to interpret phonetic spelling and diacritical marks.
- Teach the use of the dictionary to determine meanings of unknown words.
- Suggest that the student check word origins, which often provide additional associative clues.

Teach the student how to locate information in an encyclopedia.

- Teach the student how to use guide words to rapidly "zero in" on the information desired.
- Indicate the purpose of the last-volume index and the manner in which it can help the student locate information.

Expose the student to reference materials:

- the library card catalogue
- almanacs
- the telephone directory
- newspapers
- radio and TV schedules

Increasing Instructional Effectiveness

In all subject areas, relating the content presented to the student's own life is a strategy that has been proven effective. It is important that this learning principle be considered when the instructional plan for the student is developed. For example, in studying a particular historical period, the student's interest is enhanced if the discussion includes a description of the rights and responsibilities of people his own age during that period.

Using the Newspaper

Many LD adolescents who experience years of failure and frustration within an educational setting tend to associate those experiences with the "textbook" used in the mainstream classes. The teachers of these students within the integrated classroom would increase their effectiveness by using a "nonconventional" presentation of instructional material. One which is familiar to the students and one which they associate with "normalcy" is the newspaper. It may be used in association with every subject area on the secondary level. The suggestions offered represent only a sampling of the possibilities for using the newspaper as an instructional material.

The Newspaper in Language Arts
1. Parts of speech. Frequently the adolescent's speaking and writing is negatively affected through his lack of familiarity with the "parts of speech" of the English language. Reviewing can be accomplished easily using the newspaper by asking the student to read a news story and to then underline the nouns, pronouns, and verbs. Advertisements which attempt to sway the reader will provide the student with adjectives and adverbs.
2. Advertising in newspapers is concise and succinct. Using ads as models, ask students to write their own ads. An effective way of correcting these, is to have the students exchange them, deleting unnecessary words from each other's ad.
3. For the students who have severe reading problems and/or who need a "stimulus" to encourage written expression, the use of newspaper visuals is suggested. Students might be asked to:

- Pretend you are the photographer who took a particular photo. Explain why you took it and what message you hoped the picture would convey to the reader.

- Select a news photo and write a story about it.

- Select a photo and write down ten words that describe how the picture made you think or feel.

- Select a photo and write a caption that you feel best fits the picture.

4. Ask the students to skim the sports section, listing the types of action words they find. This section often is interesting to adolescents, and that interest is frequently reflected in their increased motivation to complete assignments. A related task might be to ask them to describe what they feel constitute the ingredients of a good sports story.

Study Skills
1. Outlining

Classify newspaper articles under specific headings by placing a number of articles relating to three selected topics in an envelope. Ask students to organize them according to which section of the paper they feel they are most appropriate—sports, social, advertising, etc. This may be varied or made more challenging by having the response timed. A student may graph his timed response and compare present performance to his previous efforts.

2. Finding the main idea

Cut ten articles from the newspaper. Separate the headline from the text. Read each article and locate the most suitable headline. This activity may be easily adapted to differing levels.

3. Vocabulary building

Study vocabulary in headlines and news stories concerned with sports. Make a list of synonyms found for "win" and "defeat."

4. Reading graphs and tables

Mount sample graphs and tables on tagboard. Write questions on the back to offer practice in understanding and interpretation.

5. Summarizing

Use the entertainment section of the newspaper according to the student's individual interests. For the student who is a sports fan, his assignment would be to take notes for one week on sports stories and, after this, to write a summary of his favorite team's activities. For the student who enjoys TV, he would be asked to write an evaluation of five programs.

Creative Activities

The newspaper is an effective tool to stimulate creative expression in adolescents, such as

- Writing a news story that might appear in the paper 50 years in the future.

- Selecting a picture of a person that does not have a caption. Students could then write a description of the person, his background, occupation, interests, etc.

- Dramatizing an advertisement.

- Cutting out headlines and having students write their own story to go with the headlines.

- Writing a letter to a favorite comic strip character.

Using the Newspaper in Social Studies Class

- Analyze the daily political cartoon in class discussion. Following this, ask the students to draw a cartoon of their own relating to an event being studied in social studies class.

- Have students rewrite a front page story concerning a communist country as if they worked for a newspaper in that country.

- Ask students to select a historical event and write a news article about the event as if it had happened in contemporary society.

Oral Communications

A significant factor in determining a student's educational and social success is his competence with oral communications. Effective oral communication, a learned behavior, is defined as the process of interacting through heard and spoken messages in a variety of situations.

Oral Communications Program Guidelines

1. Oral communication instruction should address the needs of students in everyday situations.
2. The classroom should be used as a learning situation.
3. Instruction should emphasize the interactive nature of speaking and listening.
4. The program goal should be that of enhancing the student's repertoire and use of effective speaking behaviors.
5. Oral communication skills can be enhanced by using parents, supportive staff, and appropriate instructional technology.
6. Communication instruction should be a clearly identifiable facet of the curriculum.
7. The program should be based on a school-wide assessment of the speaking and listening needs of students.

8. Program effectiveness is increased through in-service training of all curriculum area teachers on the development of effective communication environments in their classrooms.
9. Program emphasis should focus on specific behaviors that the student is able to change.
10. Local communications programs should be integrated at the state level to establish a resource network. Teachers interested in further information on this topic may contact:

American Speech-Language Hearing Association
10801 Rockville Pike
Rockville, Maryland 20852

Speech-Communication Association
5205 Leesburg Pike
Falls Church, Virginia 22041

MATHEMATICS

Arithmetic is a universal language, a symbolic language that allows individuals everywhere to think about, record, and communicate ideas regarding the elements and relationships of quantity. Many of the symptoms that characterize LD students have implications for learning mathematics. Children who are easily distracted, who have inadequate perceptive ability, or who have deficient motor development, may inadvertently have been denied experiences that would have allowed them to build an understanding of form, space, time, order, distance, and quantity.

Successful Math Program Ingredients

In developing any remedial math program for the LD adolescent, one must address the total student. For example, the student's chronological age, grade level, and educational prognosis must be consistent with the program's design. A number of basic ingredients should be included in a math program for the mainstreamed LD adolescent.

The program must accurately diagnose the student's deficiencies (and strengths), and be designed to ameliorate his deficiencies and build on his strengths.

The focus should be on specific concept and skill acquisition, not on normative programs and evaluation.

The program should be inherently flexible to allow for its adaptation to the needs of the individual student.

There should be a pervasive attempt to provide a math curriculum that is relevant to the "real world." Goals should be considered in terms of the individual's attaining independence in society. If math concepts are presented in relation to personal finance, comparative shopping, and consumer affairs, the student's interest and motivation increase. The student can be taught to read recipes, to measure liquids and solids, and to cut recipes in half or double them. Each new concept should be presented in a concrete manner, and introduced through direct experience wherever possible. Instruction should focus on logic and rational thought, rather than on rote memorization.

Guidelines for Presenting Math Concepts to the LD Adolescent

In attempting to adapt or modify a traditional secondary-level math curriculum, the teacher must be cognizant of the specific instructional strategies that have been found effective. The following guidelines are suggested for concept presentation.

Math concepts should be viewed in a developmental hierarchy. The educator's task is to determine (1) the range of topics (objectives) considered appropriate for instruction, and (2) the specific methodologies to be employed.

Remove reading (wherever possible) as a requirement of the arithmetic curriculum. In many math programs, as the math concepts become more difficult, the student's required reading ability increases proportionally. For the LD adolescent, this upward spiraling can be a critical problem.

Employ a variety of instructional strategies. Too often, we educators neglect to teach a student how to learn.

Change achievement evaluation from a "percentage correct" basis to a "trials-to-criterion" basis. The "percentage correct" basis of evaluation provides information only on how well the student's performance compared with his peers—a normative reference. The trials-to-criterion approach measures the degree of mastery a student has attained relative to the acquisition of a specific skill, i.e., he is evaluated against the criterion established for success (or proficiency) with the task. This is important in light of the fact that many math programs are developed on a fixed-frequency basis. This means that a certain number of pages within a math text are devoted to a specific concept without allowance given to the individual student learning rates which differ considerably.

Provide for the student's mastery of math principles and concepts. The LD student must be provided repetition and reinforcement if he is to achieve confidence in this utilization of math.

Individualization of Math Instruction

For the teacher who desires to effectively individualize math lessons on the secondary level, the following guidelines are suggested:

1. The teacher should assist the student to generalize from the specific. Whatever is learned should be generalized to many different kinds of operations (e.g., counting might include counting dissimilar objects, sides of a cube, scattered objects, etc.).
2. Each lesson should clearly establish connections between concepts.
3. The mainstreamed LD student needs practice if he is to build greater understanding and flexibility in the use of math ideas in varied situations.
4. The teacher must attempt to build the student's self-confidence. One way to achieve this objective is to present material at a level which allows the student to experience success. If the student is to succeed, the teacher must accurately assess both the student's skill level and the specific deficiencies responsible for his math difficulties.

Where to Begin with Instruction: A Task Analysis Approach

Task analysis is a vehicle that a teacher may apply to any subject area or level in order to identify definitively a starting point for instruction.

Step 1: State the ultimate task of the instructional activity; i.e., what the student is expected to perform following instruction.

Step 2: Determine what subsidiary skills are required for the student to perform the ultimate task.

Step 3: Decide which of these skills is immediately prerequisite to the ultimate task, and rank all the skills in a hierarchy.

Step 4: Construct a test to diagnose and then measure the student's knowledge of each skill in the hierarchy. It is important that the test questions be constructed so as to measure one skill at a time.

Diagnoses of a student's math skills should be made at three levels: enactive, iconic, and symbolic. The enactive is the most concrete level of functioning. If a student is operating on the enactive level, he needs manipulative aids (such as a construction-paper fraction kit) to complete a task. The iconic level is a semi-concrete cognitive processing stage. Students here need the help of diagrams to solve exercises. The symbolic level is the most desirable and abstract of the three. Here a student can reason through the use of symbols.

In developing individualized math programs for the LD students, it is essential that a primary emphasis be targeted toward the instruction of basic skills. The effectiveness of such programs are contingent upon three variables: the student, the teacher, and the educational setting.

Student Issues

- Provide for individual learning profiles. Recognize how factors of student mobility, external support, and differing entry levels affect student progress.

- Integrate affective aspects of math. Consider how the student's anxiety can be overcome how student's desire to learn math can be increased.

- Emphasize the relationship of language and math.

- Develop systems to communicate with and involve parents wherever possible.

- Relate basic skill development, concept building and problem solving in the plan.

Teacher Issues

- Appropriate levels and modes of staffing that lead to effective instruction in basic skills is a major concern.

- Explore the use of teacher aides and technology to assist teachers and enable them to direct more of their time to direct instruction of skills.

- In-service training to educate teachers on the math programs used within the school will increase their effectiveness.

Educational Institution Issues

The responsibility of the secondary schools is to produce competent high school graduates. This implies that:

- Goals and objectives must be identified and clearly articulated.

- Nondiscriminatory evaluation strategies are to be developed to measure student achievement on the stated objectives.

- A comprehensive instructional program (including basic skills) will be developed through a unified effort of all segments of the education population.

- The support of building administrators is a critical factor in the effectiveness of the program.

- The program should allow for modification as indicated through the evaluation system.

When the mainstream teacher attempts to individualize math instruction for the LD adolescent, it is important that certain factors be incorporated into the instructional plan.

Guidelines for Individualizing Math

1. Activities planned should reduce the influence of student age on successful performance.
2. The design should allow for implementation with efficient expenditure of time and effort.
3. The activities initially presented the student should begin at a point wherein he is able to experience success.
4. The individualized plan should allow for options.
5. The format of the plan, the inherent objectives, skills, etc., should be compatible and relate to the student's total educational situation.
6. Review and practice should be presented in an interesting and nondemeaning manner.
7. The program should incorporate diagnosis of the student's specific understanding of concepts and skills within the math area.

An excellent resource in the area of math individualization on the secondary level is Cawley (1975).

Once the teacher is comfortable with the design of the math program and the guidelines for its presentation, he should then focus on structuring the material in a way that will enhance the student's ability to retain learned concepts for later retrieval.

Suggestions to Enhance the LD Student's Math Retention Capacity

Each lesson's emphasis should be on "finding out." Every lesson should aim to help the student seek answers to questions, not just accumulate experiences.

An approach structured on the student's need for independence is that of contracting with LAPs.

The Learning Activity Package for Math

Collins (1975, p. 175) suggests that the following components be included in a package approach to assist the student who is having problems in math:

LAP*

Student's Unit	Teacher's Commentary
1. Procedure flow chart	1. Introduction
2. Behavioral objectives stated in language student can understand	2. Prerequisites
3. Pre-test (situational as well as paper and pencil)	3. Sequence placements
4. Activities: paper and pencil, audio tapes, films or filmstrips, laboratory experiments, references to textbooks, magazines, games, puzzles, drill and practice	4. Vocabulary
	5. Suggested required activities
	6. Objectives correlated with pre-test and activities
5. Post-test (situational as well as paper and pencil).	7. Comments on evaluation
	8. Post-test (situational as well as paper and pencil)
	9. Keys to tests and activities

This strategy allows for both individual and group presentation, may be used as an alternative to the textbook, and is adaptable to all teacher methodologies.

Materials suggested for use in teaching functional math and specific skills are presented below.

1. *Consumer and Career Mathematics*—Text—Bolston, L. Cary; Woodown, H. Douglas & Gipson, J.H. Foresmon & Co. Glenview, Ill.

   This text contains 18 chapters that deal with such topics as basic math skills, income, banking, credit, taxes, transportation, housing, insurance, purchasing, and budgeting.

---

*Reprinted with the permission of the National Council of Teachers of Mathematics. *35th Yearbook, The Slow Learner in Mathematics,* by E.A. Collins, 1975.

2. *Skills for Everyday Living*—Program—David H. Wiltail Motivational Dev. Inc., P.O. Box 427, Bishop, CA 93514

The main purpose of this program is to help students become more effective in handling situations. Students learn to find information and then to follow instructions in applying this information. Many projects require that students understand decimal fractions and percentages. Application of skills is always stressed.

Sample of topics:

Using a restaurant menu	Phone bills
Comparative shopping	Living with your income
Paying bills	Using a bus schedule

3. *Project Math*—Program—John F. Cawley Ph.D. Box 6-7, University of Connecticut, Storrs, Connecticut 06268

This program, which is the result of research and demonstration efforts, offers the teacher a comprehensive curriculum to use in the teaching of exceptional students from preschool through high school. It is comprised of lesson guides for the teaching of skills and concepts in the area of numbers and operations, sets and operations, patterns, fractions, geometry, and measurements. A comprehensive parallel system to be used in fostering verbal problem-solving skills consists of a series of laboratory experiences for the application of various arithmetic concepts in applied social settings.

This program provides the teacher with multiple options for meeting the instructional needs of exceptional students. Within the curriculum are various ways for the student to demonstrate his competence. Creative use of pictorial aids and various manipulations are encouraged throughout the program. Students are also encouraged to use math skills as a vehicle to higher cognitive processes.

Teachers are encouraged to individualize their presentations. The diagnostic/prescriptive tools and materials are included to facilitate the most effective use of material.

4. *Basic Skills in Mathematics*—Program—Russell F. Jacobs, Harcourt, Brace-Jovanovich

This is a program in fundamental operations, designed to help students master basic skills that are necessary for successful lives. It consists of four units—whole numbers, fractions, decimals, and percentages. Concepts of measurement are included, with special emphasis given to metric units.

This program is suitable for individualized or group use. Involvement of the student is encouraged. The readability is generally high, with special attention given to short words and sentences.

5. *Pacemaker Practical Arithmetic Series: Working Makes Sense; Money Makes Sense; Using Dollars and Sense*—Program—Charles H. Kahn and J. Bradley Harris

    The series explores many areas regarding the "world of work." It is a simplified series geared for the moderately disabled student who is deficient in knowledge of and experience with working, saving, and spending. It is an excellent supplement to a course geared to assisting adolescents who are seeking employment.

6. *To Buy or Not To Buy*—Melinda E. Blair, under the direction of Ralph Nader, Random House

    This learning unit helps students become aware of consumer issues. Within the classroom, students investigate the skills involved in purchasing different types of products. Through an investigation of specific purchases, students are led to an in-depth study of key consumer issues—advertising, labeling, product safety, contracts and fine print, and product and service complaints. The complete unit includes cassettes and records.

7. *Useful Arithmetic*—John Wool and Raymond J. Baker, Frank E. Richards, Co., Inc.

    A two-part series discussing practical, relevant topics that are and will be of major concern to individuals who will be entering the world of work. Topics such as grocery bills, savings bonds, sales slips, transportation costs, electric bills, and price comparisons are included. Format could be improved through a more realistic presentation, and prices need to be updated, but the information is essential.

8. *The Bank Book*—John D. Wool, Frank E. Richards, Co., Inc.

    This publication explores the various services of banks. By comparison to other publications, this program is factual and easy to follow.

9. *Let's Go Shopping*—Marge L. Landy, Frank E. Richards, Co. Inc.

    Interesting, necessary concepts in our consumer-oriented society. This program discusses the perils and confusion in today's marketplace, but unfortunately merely scratches the surface. This program has an antiquated format and distorted consumer information regarding today's market.

10. *Using Money Series*—John D. Wool, Frank E. Richards, Co., Inc.

    A four-part series: counting money, making money, buying power and earning, spending, and saving. This series attempts to prepare students to be responsible, contributing adults. Emphasis is on good money-management. The series is an appropriate supplement to a community survival course. The program may initially be used in the classroom, with a later transfer of the classes into the community. The goal is to provide the student with opportunities to apply the skills learned in real situations.

11. *Getting Ready for Pay Day*—Margaret W. Hudson & Ann H. Weaver, Frank E. Richards, Co., Inc.

A three-part series exploring with the student various aspects of checking accounts, savings accounts, and planning. The graphics are poor, but the information is necessary. This program is excellent material for the educable mentally retarded secondary student, or as a supplement for the learning disabled or emotionally disturbed adolescent.

12. *Measuring the Metric Way*—Richard Allan Log, Frank E. Richards, Co., Inc.

This program is designed to introduce students to the metric system. It includes such topics as measuring metric length, distance, speed, weight, volume, and temperature. These topics are the most common and essential for consumer survival in the coming metric world. Except for a chart at the end of the book, there is little mention of English-to-metric conversion.

13. *The Getting Along Series of Skills*—Thomas J. Mooney, Frank E. Richards Co., Inc.

A three-part series emphasizing various skills (math, reading, spelling, and word study). The major theme is how to find and keep a job in the community. An excellent idea, but the material is somewhat dated. The series is wordy. This may pose problems for the LD student who has difficulty with reading and/or a visual discrimination disability.

14. *Master Mind*—Random House

A widely acclaimed and popular game of logic and permutations. It's easy enough for primary-level children, yet challenging to adults. One player sets up four colored pegs behind a shield. His opponent tries to discover the pegs' order of placement; after each attempt, he receives information that he can use in his next try. The object is to deduce the pegs' order in as few attempts as possible.

15. *The I Hate Mathematics Book*—By Marilyn Burns, Random House Pub.

Written specifically for students who are convinced that (1) math is impossible, and (2) math is for smart kids who can't play stickball, and is no fun anyhow. This book says that math is nothing more than a way of looking at the world, that math is made up of the same stuff as any kid's life. In this 124-page book, you'll find over 200 math events, gags, magic tricks, and experiments to prove it.

16. *Mathematics Illustrated Dictionary*—Random House

There is always a need for a math dictionary that is simple to read, completely up-to-date, and well illustrated. With over 2,000 old and new math terms defined in simple language and appropriate diagrams, this 225-page, time-saving reference quickly leads readers to an understanding of math concepts and terms. Broad and complete coverage.

17. *Games & Aids for Teaching Math*—By Nikki Schreiver

A 118-page book of tear-out, ready-to-use games and puzzles to interest children in grades 3-8. The 16 games and 10 puzzles cover fractions, measurements, averages, percentages, geography, geometry, and many other topics. All are fully explained in the rules and objectives written for each game.

18. *More Games and Aids for Teaching Math*—Nikki Schreiver
    Follows the same successful format of the author's first book, but adds 18 new math games. Again, the "game book" and rules and objectives are included. There is also a particularly valuable section in this book dealing with how to organize a math game lab, library, and tournament.

Suggested Practical Activities

The teacher of the secondary-level LD student should explore the use of alternative modes of concept presentation. The use of concrete, noncommercial materials allows the student to learn concepts in a practical and motivating way.

- *Playing cards.* Skills can be gained from dealing, playing, and scoring various card games.

- *Poker chips.* Chips can be used for scoring in games, as reinforcers in a behavior modification program, or as money in a school store. The use of chips provides additional practice for the student in regrouping or borrowing operations in math.

- *Physical education.* The student can learn to measure various track and field events. This is an effective way to teach measurement and conversion from one unit to. another. A stopwatch adds another dimension in telling time.

- *Science.* The study of planets, sun, and shadows can give the student the opportunity to measure distance, while the study of temperature variations teaches the reading of a thermometer scale.

REFERENCES

Cawley, J.F. Teaching arithmetic to mentally handicapped children. In E.L. Meyer, G.A. Vergason, and R.J. Whelan (Eds.), *Strategies for teaching exceptional children.* Denver: Love Publishing Co., 1975, pp. 250-263.

Collins, E.A. The slow learner in mathematics. In Lowry, W.C. (Ed.), *35th Yearbook of the National Council of Teachers of Mathematics.* Washington, .D.C.: NCTM, 1975.

Fry, E. *Teaching faster reading.* New York: Cambridge University Press, 1963.

Miller, W.H. *Diagnosis and correction of reading difficulties in secondary school students.* New York: The Center for Applied Research in Education, Inc., 1973.

SUGGESTED READINGS

Bartel, N. Problems in arithmetic achievement. In D. Hammill and N. Bartel (Eds.), *Teaching children with learning and behavior problems.* Boston: Allyn and Bacon, Inc., 1975, pp. 61-88.

Buswell, G.T., & John, L. *Diagnostic chart for individual difficulties. Fundamental processes in arithmetic.* Indianapolis: Bobbs-Merrill.

Cawley, J.F., Fitzmaurice, A.M., Goodstein, H.A., Lepore, A.U., Sedlak, R., & Althans, V. *Project MATH, Level I.* Tulsa, Okla.: Educational Progress, A Division of Educational Development Corporation, 1976.

Cawley, J.F. and Vitello, S.J. Model for arithmetical programming for handicapped children. *Exceptional Children,* 1972, *39,* 101-110.

Connolly, A.J., Nachtman, W., & Pritchett, E.M. *Key Math.* Circle Pines, Minn.: American Guidance Service.

Deschant, E. *Diagnosis and remediation of reading disability.* New York: Parker Publishing Co., Inc., 1968.

Hammill, D.D., & Bartel, N. *Teaching children with learning and behavior problems.* Boston: Allyn and Bacon, Inc., 1974.

Johnson, D., & Myklebust, H.R. *Learning disabilities: Educational principles and practices.* New York: Grune and Stratton, 1967.

Lerner, J. *Children with learning disabilities.* Boston: Houghton Mifflin, 1971.

Myers, P.L. and Hammill, D.D. *Methods for learning disorders.* New York: Wiley, 1969.

Smith, R. *Clinical teaching.* New York: McGraw-Hill, 1974.

Sobel, M.A. Providing for the slow learner in the junior high school. *The Mathematics Teacher,* 1959, *52,* 347-353.

Waugh, R.P. Relationship between modality preference and performance. *Exceptional Children,* 1973, *39,* 465-469.

Williams, J.P. Learning to read: A review of theories and models. *Reading Research Quarterly,* 1973, *8,* 121-146.

Ysseldyke, J.E., & Salvia, J. Diagnostic-prescriptive teaching: Two models. *Exceptional Children,* 1974, *40,* 181-186.

Chapter 5

Career and Vocational Programs

5

The term "learning-disabled" describes students of various abilities, accomplishments, and aspirations. Educators must avoid stereotyping these students' career options because of misconceptions of their occupational potential.

Career planning for the LD student should include instruction in marketable skills that relate to many different career options. The employability of the LD student is enhanced by identifying his occupational strengths, then matching them to specific job requirements (Wiij, 1972, Brutter, 1966).

The teacher must deal with the LD student's emotional and social difficulties—which may interfere with job performance and employability—as well as with his specific occupational concerns (Williamson 1974-75).

CAREER ED MODELS

Vocational Entry Skills Model

Washburn (1975) sought to develop career-education programs for the LD adolescent. Her model—which emphasizes "Vocational Entry Skills"—includes such facets as:

- vocational academics, survival reading, writing, spelling, and math relevant to daily life;

- vocational physical education to help the student develop fine-motor and coordination skills;

99

- vocational "know how" training in the skills required to obtain and keep a desirable job. The student is given experience with interviews, résumés, money, transportation, driver education, personality development, and personal problem solving;

- vocational entry skills instruction designed to develop basic work skills required for job success through "hands on" experience, and to develop general work skills and appropriate attitudes toward work; and

- placement of the student in job situations through volunteer work, work experiences, and job placement.

Teacher Counseling Model

Another prominent career educator (Williamson, 1974-75) takes a broader view: her approach emphasizes alternatives for the LD student through effective teacher counseling. She stresses the need to shift the emphasis of the secondary-level curriculum from remediating the student's deficits to capitalizing on his strengths. She suggests viewing service vocations as particularly promising for the LD adolescent.

Work/Study Approach

Koppitz (1971), in a five-year follow-up study of LD students, recommends that vocational programs for this group include one or two years of vocational training and the study of basic skills, followed by one to two years of skills training in a work/study program.

An Integrated Approach

A career preparation program must primarily take into account the student's ability to accept direction, his ability to work independently, his attendance record, and the safety of his work habits.

At the same time a student is experiencing an occupation first-hand (working in a shop, for instance), his academic instruction should focus on that occupation's vocabulary, the mathematics and reading skills it requires, and the occupation itself (working conditions, duties, required knowledge). This approach integrates, for the LD student, essential concepts and an experience base.

According to 1976 statistics from the U.S. Department of Labor, 83 percent of the jobs that will be available in the next ten years will not require a four-year college education, but will demand some specialized education and training. Adolescents with specific learning disabilities who are offered only traditional, academic programs will be denied these jobs—yet LD students, in fact, constitute a top-priority population with whom to explore the alternative of career education.

The "Work-Ed" Program

A model career-education program that has succeeded with both normal and exceptional adolescents was developed in New Jersey. (Hackettstown, 1977) The two major components of this "Work-Ed" Program are communication courses and career guidance.

Communication courses strive to assure that the student acquires skill proficiency which matches his own capability. The student's tasks include interviewing for jobs, filling out employment applications, writing résumés, and reading for the purpose of career research. These activities are important, as the LD student must be shown what his behavior is really like (i.e., how he appears to an observer). The student should also be given specific instruction in skills that will make him more socially acceptable. This goal may be achieved through a "values clarification" segment that is designed to help the student become aware of who he is and what his goals are, thus enabling him to select a suitable career to reach those goals.

Career guidance deals with the student's interests and abilities. Career-guidance techniques include testing, group counseling, and individual counseling. Career evaluation of the LD student should not be viewed as an exclusively external phenomenon; it is equally important that the adolescent engage in self-evaluation if he is to choose realistic career goals. The student should be encouraged to be flexible in contemplating career or vocational choices.

The underlying rationale of the Work-Ed approach is that each person has the capacity to find fulfillment and job satisfaction. This fulfillment, however, is dependent on the student's knowledge of both society's needs and his own. Both sets of needs should be explored.

PRINCIPLES OF CAREER EDUCATION

Dr. Sidney P. Marland, Jr., former United States Commissioner of Education, wrote in 1971: "All education is career education—or should be. I propose that a universal goal of American education, starting now, be this—that every young person completing his school program at grade 12 be ready to enter either higher education or useful and rewarding employment" (p. 22).

Williamson (1975) has outlined four issues that must be addressed if career education is to be implemented successfully:

1. Career education must emphasize development of basic literacy skills.
2. Career education must provide numerous career options to students, including the alternative of college attendance.
3. Career education must offer insightful guidance in career options, rather than limit itself to vocational training.
4. Career education must be researched as a viable alternative to present educational programs for secondary-school LD students.

In developing vocational opportunities for the LD adolescent the teacher must include the following three ingredients in his educational plan:

1. Consideration of the abilities and interests of the student. The teacher must first discover what the student can do.
2. Follow-up with "hands on" opportunities, so that the student can practice the skills learned in the classroom.
3. Reality-based job preparation.

TEACHER RESPONSIBILITY IN CAREER PLANNING

It is important for the teacher to analyze both the student and the proposed career area.

Job Analysis

In a task analysis of the job, the teacher should:

1. get a specific, comprehensive description of the job;
2. analyze the major tasks involved in performing the job;
3. present a task to the student only after the teacher has delineated the required sequence of performance, identified the student's required behavioral response, and adjusted the task to allow for any problems created by the student's disability; and clearly state learning objectives, including the conditions under which the job is to be performed, the behavior required, and the required proficiency level of each job skill.

Student Analysis

The teacher should identify the general characteristics of the individual student with regard to:

- attitudes
- interests
- motivation
- educational level
- physical nature

The teacher's task here is to incorporate in vocational planning the student's individuality and his specific learning disability. A Student Inventory from the New Jersey State Department of Education's Vocational Manual is easily administered to the adolescent, and may significantly help the teacher ascertain the student's interests and career awareness. (See Appendix F.)

By combining the results of a job analysis and a student analysis, the teacher can develop an effective, individualized vocational learning package.

Occupational Knowledge Objectives

In developing a vocational/career program for an LD adolescent, the teacher should strive to:

- identify sources of information which may lead to employment
- define occupational categories in terms of required education and job experience
- know the minimum requirements of given occupations
- prepare job applications and interviews
- know standards of behavior for various types of employment
- know the legal aspects of employment
- understand aspects of employment (other than financial) that would affect the individual's satisfaction with a job

Task Elements

In addressing these objectives, the teacher must consider the specific tasks involved in an occupation (job) and determine each task's elements.

There are three ingredients inherent in any task:

1. *Concepts and knowledge*—the basic concepts an individual must comprehend in order to perform the task successfully.
2. *Skills*—the physical (psychomotor) requirements necessary to execute the task successfully.
3. *Abilities*—the specific abilities necessary to learn the task or perform it adequately.

An example of task analysis as it relates to a specific task requiring the student to synthesize information is contained in Exhibit 5-1.

Exhibit 5-1 Task Analysis

The task is to complete a job application form.

Concepts and Knowledge Required
  Ability to understand the requested information
  Ability to provide the requested information

Skills Required
  Ability to record information accurately, and clearly
  Ability to follow written instruction

Abilities
  Ability to read the directions
  Ability to adhere to task (complete the form)

The Basic Skills

The eight general areas which comprise task skills are

1. cognitive skills
2. affective (social) skills
3. psychomotor skills
4. perceptual skills
5. verbal skills
6. language skills
7. quantitative skills
8. occupational aptitudes

Developing an Instructional Plan

The skills necessary to any task's successful completion must be addressed in planning any career plan for an LD student. The plan should include:

- a statement of objectives that specifies the cognitive skills the student must acquire as a prerequisite to the technical skills acquisition;

- identification of the technical skills the learner must develop during the instruction;

- definition of the specific content (i.e., What is to be undertaken?);

- description of the activities that the learner will experience, under the direction and guidance of the teacher, to achieve the stated objectives;

- identification of the materials, equipment, etc., that will be used in the instructional activities;

- a system for evaluating the student's performance regarding the objectives and skills listed in the educational plan.

Whatever instructional plan the teacher develops should reflect a skills approach, an integrated program and individualization relative to the student's disability. Kimbrell and Vinegard offer excellent suggestions in *Succeeding in the World of Work* (1975).

Basic Career/Occupational Skills

It is essential that teachers be conversant with the basic skills that individuals require to function as independent adults in specific jobs. Occupational education for the handicapped should give consideration to the basic skills required in specific tasks—behaviorally as well as cognitively. These skills should be presented in a sequential order.

Skills Sequencing Principles

Four principles that a teacher involved with career-related instruction should consider following are:

1. *Interest sequencing*—involves selecting tasks in which the learner has an interest. This should be used as an initial introduction to career instruction.
2. *Logical sequencing*—suggests that the nature of the task and the prerequisite skills at each step of the task dictate the order in which skills will be addressed.
3. *Skill sequencing*—involves presenting skills in a hierarchy that are essential to performing a job.
4. *Graduated sequencing*—involves presenting material to a student in a predetermined manner that takes the student from "where he's at" to a "more advanced" or "more refined" level of functioning. For the learning-disabled student, it is essential that an accurate determination be made of the functioning level of the student relative to the concepts and/or material to be learned. Once this is completed, the teacher's task is to direct the student from: the known to the unknown; the simple to the more complex; the practical to the theoretical; and the concrete to the abstract. Johnson and Johnson (1970) have identified seven commonly used graduated sequencing principles from which the above teacher's task was derived. Mager and Beach (1967) is also an excellent resource in this area.

How to Improve the Delivery of Career Services

Both relevant and sequential inservice and preservice training must be provided for regular and special education teachers at all levels.

The community, labor, business, and industry must collaborate with education in developing a curriculum that is technically appropriate and realistic in its goals for students.

We must improve our methods of forecasting labor needs, in order to avoid the waste and frustration of youths that result from oversupply of workers and undersupply of jobs.

We must stop implying that career education will solve social problems (such as environmental abuse, drug abuse, and declining test scores).

We must objectively assess the outcomes of career education, and document that where career education is systematically implemented, the academic growth of students improves.

We must seek, through self-monitoring and evaluation, the catalyst that will aggregate the power of business, labor, government, industry, education, the public, and students to produce effective career education.

Looking for a Job

The LD adolescent must be provided direct instruction on how to apply to the "real world" the behaviors they have acquired in the classroom. Kimbrell and Vinegard offer many suggestions (1975). One tool is a Learning Activity Packet, as in Exhibit 5-2.

Exhibit 5-2 Looking for a Job

A Learning Activity Packet

This packet is designed to help you get a job. It outlines in easy-to-follow steps what you should do in getting a job. It is important that you follow the steps in the order they are presented.
Proceed: follow all instructions.

Step 1. Check the "Help Wanted" ads in your local newspaper.
Read the ads carefully and use the following suggestions in answering the ads that interest you:
    a. Reply to those ads that allow you to telephone for an interview. It also permits you to ask specific questions.
    b. Consider those ads that ask you to come in for an interview. This allows you an opportunity to "sell yourself."
    c. Select those ads that require a written reponse and prepare a letter.

Exhibit 5-2 continued

Step 2. Write a basic letter of application.

To do this, follow these steps:

    a. Invest in stationery. A solid simple color is best. Your letter should look business-like and remember this letter introduces you.

    b. Use ink. Don't use a pen with a thick felt tip or any ink color other than black or blue.

    c. Decide what you are going to say in advance so that your letter is brief and clear.

    d. Never cross out anything. It is a wise investment of your time to present the letter to a prospective employer in the best form possible.

Step 3. If you need further assistance, study these line-by-line instructions:

    A. Start this information at the center of the page, going to the right of the page.

> Your name and street address
> Your city, state, and zip code
> The date

    B. On the next line, at the left margin (use a margin of about one inch), give the name and address of the person to whom you are writing.

    C. Next write the words: "Dear Sir,", "Dear Madam,", or, if you don't know who will receive your letter, "Dear Sir or Madam,";

    D. Start your letter:

> I am writing in answer to your advertisement of (fill in the date) in the (fill in the newspaper's name).

    E. Next give the reasons why you think you qualify for the position.

This paragraph should include your educational background, your skills, and your previous experiences. Also include some personal information about yourself. Be sure to state your age.

    F. End the body of the letter with some statement that shows your interest in the job.

    G. End with the words "Sincerely yours," or "Very truly yours,"; sign your name below.

    H. Take all the time you need to write a good letter. Remember that this letter is the only way that the employer can know you. It is your introduction.

    I. Keep a copy of the letter, so that you can rewrite it whenever you wish to answer an ad.

    J. Don't give up if your first efforts fail to get you the job you want. The people who succeed are those who keep trying.

> Your letter should look something like this:

Exhibit 5-2 continued

---

10 Sparrow Lane
Adams, New York 06095
January 5, 1980

Mr. John Henry
10 Margin Street
Adams, New York 06095

Dear Sir:

I am writing in answer to your advertisement of January 3 in the Metro News.

I have been a grocery clerk for two summers and a newspaper boy for three years.

I am a 16-year-old junior and enjoy doing a variety of jobs.

I hope you will grant me an interview so that we may discuss this matter further.

Sincerely yours,
[your signature]
Tommy Andrews

Step 4. Get in touch with employment agencies.

The largest agency is run by the federal government, and is called the United States Employment Service. There are also many private employment agencies.

Step 5. Talk to friends and relatives.

Ask those close to you to keep your job-hunting in mind. Personal referrals have proven an effective route to employment.

Step 6. Be on the lookout for new employment opportunities.

New companies, factories, or stores opening in your area bring with them many new jobs.

When you have completed all previous steps in this packet, take the following test.

"Steps to Getting a Job" Test
1. What are the different ways employers ask you to contact them when you answer their ads?
2. What information do you need before writing a letter of application for a job?
3. Obtain a copy of the "Help Wanted" ads in your local newspaper. Write (but don't mail) a letter of application to two of them. Check your letter against the suggestions.

Using Career Education in the Subject Areas

Goals: To develop writing skills, with specific focus on letter-writing skills and paragraph formation.

Simulation Game

Simulation is an excellent activity to stimulate student thinking and to provide a forum for student discussion.

Activity:
1. Divide the class into small groups.
2. Students choose a company to study from the "Yellow Pages" of the phone book.
3. Each group simulates the personnel department of this company.
4. The group members brainstorm to develop a list of the type of jobs and staff members their "company" needs.
5. Each student writes a letter to the company requesting information on the types of positions available. Provide students with the following guidelines for writing their letters.

   • In the first paragraph, tell the person you are writing (a) who you are, (b) your grade, (c) your school, (d) what you are studying, and (e) why you would like this information.

   • In the second paragraph, explain that you need (a) information on each of the jobs available in the company, (b) descriptions of the work that people who are holding each job do, (c) salary levels, (d) skill requirements, and (e) advancement possibilities.

   • Request any posters or brochures the company uses for advertising.

After receiving these materials, each "company" sets up its employment offices, and advertises for help. Then each personnel department gives a short talk on its job openings, and starts interview sessions.

SUMMARY

Career and vocational programs for the learning disabled student should enable him to enjoy a broad continuum of options by providing him with marketable skills for a receptive market.

REFERENCES

Kimbrell, G., & Vinegard, B.S. *Succeeding in the world of work.* Bloomington, Ill.: McKnight Publishing Co., 1975.

Koppitz, E.M. *Children with learning disabilities: A five year follow-up study.* New York: Grune and Stratton, 1971.

Marland, S.P., Jr. Career education. *Today's Education,* 1971, *60,* 22-25.

Washburn, W.Y. Where to go in vocational education for secondary LD students. *Academic Therapy.* 1975, *11,* 31-35.

Wiij, E. The emerging LD crisis. *Journal of Rehabilitation,* 1972, *38,* 15-17.

Williamson, A.P. Career education: Implications for secondary LD students. *Academic Therapy.* (Winter 1974-1975), *10,* 193-200.

Work-Ed (World of Related Knowledge and Educational Development). Project No. 72-468 Title III-IVC-ESEA. Hackettstown, N.J.: State Department of Education, 1977.

SUGGESTED READINGS

Bailey, L.I., & Stadt, W. *Career education: New approaches to human development.* Bloomington, Ill.: McKnight Publishing Co., 1973.

Brutter, M. Vocational education of the brain-injured adolescent and young adult at the Vanguard School. *An international approach in learning disabilities of children and youth. Proceedings of the Third Annual Conference of the ACLD.* Tulsa, Okla.: 1966.

Buontempo, G., McNulty, T., & Ringelheim, D. *Vocational education for the handicapped.* Trenton, N.J.: Department of Education, 1974.

Butler, R.L., & York, E.G. Career education now. *The Vocational Guidance Quarterly.* March 1972, *20* (3), 188-192.

Cegelka, P.T. Sex role stereotyping in special education—A look at secondary work study programs. *Exceptional Children,* 1973, *39,* 541-546.

Colella, H.V. Career development center: A modified high school for the handicapped. *Teaching Exceptional Children,* 1973, *5,* 110-118.

Cowles, A., Condon, R.W., Falkner, J.F., & Jackson, S. *Pre-vocational preparation of exceptional children and youth in the city of Everett, Washington.* Everett, Washington: Everett School District, 1967. (ERIC Document Reproduction Service No. ED 012526).

Ginzberg, E. *Career guidance.* New York: McGraw-Hill Book Co., 1971.

Handbook for career guidance counselors. Urbana, Ill.: University of Illinois, 1975.

Heir, E.L. *Review and synthesis of foundations for career education.* Columbus, Ohio: ERIC Clearinghouse on Vocational and Technical Education, 1972.

Heir, E.L. *Review and synthesis of foundations for career education.* Washington, D.C.: Office of Education, 1972.

Iwine, P. *Exploratory occupational education for LD adolescents.* Paper presented at "LD in the Secondary School." A symposium sponsored by the Montgomery County Intermediate Unit, Norristown, Pa., March 1975.

Johnson, S.P., & Johnson, R.R. *Developing individualized instructional material.* Oak Lawn, Ill.: Westinghouse Learning Corp., 1970.

Kimbrell, G., & Vinegard, B.S. *Succeeding in the world of work.* Bloomington, Ill.: McKnight Publishing Co., 1975.

Klapper, M., & Neff, W.S. *Vocational readiness for young disabled students in New York City. A 3-year interim report of a 5-year collaborative study.* Albany, N.Y.: New York State Education Department, 1966.

Mager, R.F., & Bench, J.M., Jr. *Developing vocational instructions.* Belmont, Calif.: Fearon Publishers, 1967.

Mason, R.E. & Haines, P.G. *Cooperative occupational educational and work experience in the curriculum.* Danville, N.Y.: Interstate Printers and Publishers, 1965.

Matters, C.H. Serving the handicapped and disadvantaged in special programs. *American Vocational Journal,* 1974, *49,* 34-35.

McClure, L., & Baum, C. (Eds.). *Essays on career education.* Portland, Ore.: Northwest Regional Educational Laboratory, 1973.

McClure, L., & Baum, C. (Eds.). *New directions in career education: school, employer, and home based models.* Washington, D.C.: U.S. Department of Health, Education and Welfare, 1972.

Miller, S., Lotsof, A.B., & Miller, T. *Survey of secondary program needs and directions.* Unpublished report, 1976.

U.S. Department of Labor. *Dictionary of occupational titles, Volumes I and II, 1965.* Washington, D.C.: U.S. Government Printing Office, 1965.

U.S. Department of Labor. *Supplement of the occupational outlook handbook, 1974-75.* Washington, D.C.: U.S. Government Printing Office, 1974.

Work-Ed (World of Related Knowledge and Educational Development). Project No. 72-468 Title III-IVC-ESEA. Hackettstown, N.J.: State Department of Education, 1977.

Chapter 6

Effective Teaching through Affective Education

6

Each LD adolescent is a complex and unique being. To provide him effective instruction, the teacher must consider his feelings, attitudes, and self-esteem—not just his level of cognitive functioning.

A teacher is responsible for the emotional climate in his classroom, and this climate is inseparable from effective teaching.

PROFILE OF THE EFFECTIVE TEACHER

In setting the stage for learning, a teacher must accept the fact that he is the single most significant variable in the learning situation. Although it is recognized in education that there is no single teacher "type" that is most effective, there do appear to be some traits that all effective teachers share.

The effective teacher never forgets that the student must be the focus in the educational process. Thus, this teacher never pontificates or speaks primarily for self-enhancing motives.

The effective teacher never pretends to be something he isn't. Adolescents are extremely perceptive and sensitive to the feelings expressed by adults. If the student feels that the teacher is "trying to put one over on me," the teacher's credibility suffers, and so does his potential effectiveness with the student.

The effective teacher never creates "win/lose" situations. This phenomenon occurs when the teacher interacts with the adolescent in a dogmatic manner.

The effective teacher never makes self-fulfilling prophecies. The teacher who labels or stereotypes students limits the adolescent's potential. When we expect, we usually receive.

The effective teacher never forgets that teaching is not judging. The teacher should view himself as an enabler. Facilitating a student's growth demands a teacher who neither "assumes" nor "presumes" anything about either himself or his student.

The effective teacher never gives "mixed messages" that create confusion and uncertainty in the student. Teacher communication with the LD adolescent should always be clear. Verbal messages should be congruent with the messages conveyed through body language.

The effective teacher deals with the present. The teacher should not expend valuable time and energy seeking the etiology of a student's behavior, but should focus on present behavior with an eye to improving it.

The effective teacher does not negatively manipulate the child. A teacher should never behave with the intention of generating guilt or shame in his students.

CREATING A CLIMATE FOR LEARNING

A teacher should determine what type of classroom environment he wants to create and what behaviors he wishes students to demonstrate within that environment.

The Teacher as Facilitator of Positive Self-Esteem

Glasser (1965) has stated that there are two needs which all human beings seek to satisfy in life—the need to love and to be loved and the need to feel worthwhile. Satisfying these needs is difficult for any adolescent who is struggling to "find himself" and establish his identity. For the LD adolescent—whose search is contaminated and slowed by feelings of unworthiness engendered by academic failure—satisfaction is virtually impossible without adult assistance. The teacher's task is to facilitate the student's movement toward positive self-esteem in an academic setting.

A teacher should be accepting of a student wherever he finds the adolescent to be functioning behaviorally. The student's "problem" behavior should be separated from any overall evaluation of the student as a person. Operationally, the teacher should be careful to comment only on the specific inappropriate behavior at hand, so that the adolescent does not feel that the teacher's negative comments reflect the teacher's estimation of the student as a person. A teacher should limit his feedback to the situation—not to the person in that situation.

Guiding Facilitative Principles

In general, be wary of making "absolute" statements, which allow the student to easily ignore your message. A statement such as "You're always late to class."

allows the student to respond with "No I'm not. Last Tuesday I was on time.", or "You're wrong. I'm not late every day, only sometimes." Thus the student effectively shifts the focus of discussion from his tardiness to your defense of the absolute "always" in your statement. You are better advised in handling a student's late arrival to class to speak with him after class or during study hall, when there will not be an audience. In this conversation, you should specifically state why his late arrival disturbs you (e.g., tardiness is disruptive to lessons, and the tardy student misses valuable information). Exhibit 6-1 illustrates how such a conversation should proceed.

You should be careful not to "hook" your feedback to a student into his past behavior. Teachers often set themselves up as victims through their own inability to remain in the present. They fall prey to this error even when they consciously attempt to relate positively to a student. A teacher may say, for example: "John, I'm glad that you're getting to class on time now, and not coming in late as you used to." Here a well-meaning teacher has effectively negated any positive reinforcement of the student's punctuality by reminding him of his previous inappropriate behavior. If you expect a student to put aside negative and inappropriate behavior, you should be careful not to resurrect that behavior.

A human being's task is to preserve his integrity. Yet every day—in countless classrooms—the only integrity that is maintained is the teacher's. Effective teaching does *not* require that you deny or suppress your own feelings; it *does* require that you deal with and express your feelings in a way that fosters the student's

Exhibit 6-1 Suggested Student Conferencing Dialogue

Teacher: "John, I'm concerned (upset, annoyed, etc.) at the number of times you've arrived late for class."
Message: Here you have clearly identified for the student the effect his behavior has upon you as a person.
Teacher: "You are missing out on some important directions."
Message: Here you have identified the effect his behavior has upon his own ability to perform.
Teacher: "Let's discuss how we can work together to get you to class on time."
Message: You have now involved him in the solution to the problem. Collaborative decision making is one of the most effective strategies for dealing with adolescents who are frequently "put off" by adults who tell them what to do.

growth. Many teachers expect respect from their students, but respond with anything but a genuine regard for the student's "dignity." Sarcasm and insults permeate many secondary-school classes. Abusive comments—such as "Glad you chose to favor us with a minute of your attention"—set the stage for a defensive "come-back" from the adolescent who feels under the teacher's verbal gun.

In general, you must focus on whatever is positive in a situation. If you reward appropriate behavior, the student is more likely to maintain and even strengthen that behavior. Little attention in teacher training programs is given to the "how to" of meshing educational goals with behavioral strategies. Yet, effectiveness is very much dependent on this integration. Hewett (1975), in a technical report on teacher attitudes toward mainstreaming, wrote:

> In general, selection of [these] behavioral goals is based on a desire to aid the child in changing maladaptive to adaptive behavior. At best, these concepts of "maladaptive" and "adaptive" provide only the broadest of guidelines for selection of specific behavioral goals. In this sense the powerful methodology of the behavior modification approach is not matched by concern with goals in learning. Teachers are provided with an efficient means of taking emotionally-disturbed children some- place, but not substantially aided in the selection of where to go. (p. 523)

Learning and motivation are influenced not only by things as they are, but also by each student's perceptions and evaluations of both his world and himself. Psychologists and educators generally agree that self-concept is a learned be- havior. Feedback that an individual receives from significant persons in his life is instrumental in shaping his sense of self-worth. Thus, if a student's motivation to learn manifests itself in terms of how he sees himself, those of us who teach must become instruments of positive feedback.

HOW TO IMPROVE TEACHER EFFECTIVENESS

As a teacher, you cannot be effective and feel good about yourself unless you teach attentive and interested students. You must carefully structure educational change if it is to produce positive results. Apply positive reinforcement consis- tently and objectively, and you can bring about dramatic progress in the LD adolescent.

Involve the student as an active participant in the educational process. Relate content to the student's world.

Allow for discussions, panels, etc., within the classroom. One of the least effective—yet, ironically, most commonly used—teaching methods is the lecture. Explore other methods.

Consider "student teaming" as an option in independent studies and projects. This approach increases student interest and socialization within the class. It is important that the teams be carefully designated after considering the dynamics which exist between the players.

Look at your own communications and at yourself as a vital ingredient in the student's learning. You must be a social psychologist to succeed with adolescents. The teacher, who is trying to improve his effectiveness, typically looks to external resources (e.g., finding the "right material," taking the "right course," etc.), while the answer usually lies in introspection.

Strive for effective communication—communication that produces the desired effect on students.

Rules for Effective Communication

Rule 1: Listen.
Cue your students that you are open to receiving messages.

Face the student and give him your complete attention. There is nothing more frustrating for the adolescent than to feel insignificant because a well-meaning teacher tries to tidy up a desk while carrying on a conversation with him.

Allow an adolescent to finish what he is saying. It is important that you clearly understand the intent of a conversation. If, for example, the purpose of the meeting is to work through a behavior problem, don't attempt to correct the student's grammar. Conversely, if the talk concerns an academic issue, don't contaminate the message by bringing the student's behavior into the dialogue.

Rule 2: Paraphrase.
Paraphrase is a skill used with great effectiveness by clinicians and therapists, but is infrequently employed by educators. By paraphrasing the student's statements, you are indicating to the student that you are listening, you understand, you care, and—most importantly—you wish to respond with accuracy to their message.

You can lead into a paraphrasing response with such openings as "Do you mean . . . ," "Do I understand correctly that . . . ," "I read you that . . . ," and "Are you saying that. . . ."

Rule 3: Check your perceptions.
There is a story of a kindergarten child who caused his teacher much concern because all of his drawings were in black and brown. The social worker, psycholo-

gist, and principal who were brought in for consultation were alarmed. All felt sure that this indeed was a "troubled child." One day the child showed a brown-and-black picture to the teacher's aide, who said, "What a nice picture! Why did you use those particular colors?" To which the child responded: "Those are the only colors in my crayon box!"

"Perception" is the meaning we impart to stimuli or events. It is a function of past experiences. You should seek to "check out" what you "think" the adolescent is feeling. You may lead into perception-checking with such phrases as "You seem to be . . . ," "I get the impression that . . . ," "You appear to be . . . ," "It sounds to me as if you are . . . ," and "From here it seems as if you are. . . ."

This is an effective technique for initiating a dialogue with an adolescent.

Rule 4: Adjust the dialogue from abstract to concrete, and vice versa.

This communication skill is of particular importance in relation to LD students, many of whom do not automatically draw conclusions or generalizations from conversations. A simple rule is to provide two specifics for every abstraction and an abstraction for every cluster of specifics.

Rule 5: Describe behavior.

For the student who experiences difficulty drawing appropriate inferences, you should provide clear descriptions of what is occurring in a dynamic situation.

These five rules should be supplemented by congruent messages, i.e., verbal and behavioral compatibility. Comprehension is also enhanced if you repeat key points.

Whatever the specific content of a conversation, be sure that you've got the facts straight and that your ideas are reasonable. Your effectiveness increases if the student sees you as believable and trustworthy.

Take personal responsibility for your messages by using the pronouns "I," "my," and "me."

How to Develop Teacher Support Systems

In addition to developing effective modes of talking with students, teachers must address the equally important issue of collegial communication. This communication entails the development of support systems and teamsmanship among those responsible for providing educational services for mainstreamed LD adolescents.

Teachers are effective when they feel they can communicate openly with their colleagues, when they share a living philosophy of education, and when they help each other.

The effectiveness of mainstream programs is dependent on trusting interdisciplinary relationships. Group cohesion can be developed in many ways, one of the most successful being the group work model developed by Lowell Tornquist. Among the activities used in this model to facilitate improved interpersonal interaction is one called "Whips." It is a lively, easily implemented "sharing" technique which may be used with adolescent students as well as a way to "break the ice" with teacher groups.

How to "Run" a Successful Group

In whatever activity the group engages, certain rules must be consistently observed by the teacher when acting as a facilitator of a students' group.

Participation should not initially be required of the adolescent. The student should say "I pass" each time it is his turn if he chooses to pass. This tactic in effect places the responsibility of the student's "passing" behavior on the other group members—they will quickly comment if anyone passes too often, and good discussions about peer group pressure can come out of this situation.

The leader should participate in the activities whenever possible and must answer any questions asked him as part of the activity. Serving as a model of the desired behavior is important. The leader should go last, however, since some students tend to echo the leader in an attempt to win his approval.

All members must show respect for one another.

The leader should not be judgmental. This is achieved by reflecting on what the group member has said ("So you are saying . . .," "Are you saying . . ."). Commenting on behavior patterns that you observe—without adding any value judgment of that behavior —is effective ("It's interesting that you . . .").

Group Work Model Activities*

Whips: Getting to know the teacher in the room next door by using this simple technique of quick verbal exercises called Whips.

- *Proud Whip.* Each team member shares with the team something he has done or something he owns that he is particularly proud of, and tells why he is proud of it.

- *Name Whip.* Each team member tells his name to the team and tells what it means to him.

- *Hero Whip.* Each member answers the question: "If you could be someone else in history, movies, etc., who would you choose to be and why."

Source: Center for Applied Instruction. Lowell Tornquist, Director. Southwest Minnesota College. Used with permission of the Center for Applied Instruction.

Paired Interviews: Another activity that has proven successful in developing open working relationships is the paired interview.

Choose a member of your team whom you do not know well. It is your task to find out in an interview as much about your partner as possible. Ask any questions you wish, and take notes. The person being interviewed has the right to refuse to answer any question. After a ten-minute interview, return to the group and tell about the person in an informed manner. The participants then change roles and repeat the procedure.

Teaching the Adolescent to Communicate

Conversation is in part self-expression. It is a way for the student to assert his individuality, tell the world how he feels, or simply "let off steam." Conversation also links people together, and is perhaps the most important single factor in improving human relations.

At its best, conversation means the pooling of information, the sharing of interests, and the bringing together of ideas.

Topics of Conversation

Topics that students might begin with include sports, books, movies, TV programs, news events, and local problems. Students may swap stories, share observations, and express opinions. Students should understand that their reactions to ideas may be more important to the conversation than the topic itself, and should thus be encouraged to express their feelings and opinions about the topics being discussed.

How to Find a Topic

Suggest that each student circle or tear out a news item that interests him. If memory is a problem for the student, ask that he keep a notebook or card-file to store such items.

Ask each student to read up on topics that are of particular interest to him. *The Reader's Guide to Periodical Literature,* available at public libraries, can help the student find articles on almost any subject.

Students should be encouraged to analyze their conversations for topic areas. In addition, they should be encouraged to practice listening, and to be prepared to report what topics were covered and how they were presented in conversation.

Ask each student to jot down a list of possible topics from his past reading and listening activities. Suggest through discussion and role playing how a student could have used some of the topics, as well as why he didn't use them if he had the opportunity.

Communicating with Parents

In order to maximize instructional effectiveness with the LD adolescent, his parents must be involved in his education. Communication with parents should be clear, consistent, supportive, and succinct.

Parent Conference Guidelines

Let parents know what will be covered in the conference in specific terms. For example, rather than inviting parents to school to discuss their child's "change in attitude over the last two weeks," say that the purpose of the meeting is to discuss "your child's indifference, as manifested through incomplete assignments."

Remove threat and anxiety from the situation. Arrange the conference room so that you are seated with the parents. Be sure to talk to both parents.

Avoid educational jargon. Put the essence of your remarks in terms parents will understand.

Be cautious in discussing other children's problems, other parents, or other teachers. Avoid judgmental terms. To do otherwise either causes parent alienation or reinforces the parents' negative feelings about their child's behavior.

Highlight the child's positive behaviors at the beginning of the conference. Make a list of these behaviors so that they can be stated definitively. "I like the way Joey gets along with his classmates," you might say. "What I'm concerned about is his progress in math."

Be specific in defining the problem. Indicate the instructional materials you are using.

Specific information provided to the parents should also include the amount of work completed by the student and the degree to which the teacher's academic expectations were met. In addition, the teacher should highlight, in the conference, the quality of the student's work.

Offer a recommendation, e.g., "Joey's math teacher has offered to provide additional assistance during study hall."

Have a file of the child's work ready to show the parents. Comparative samples are always helpful.

Provide parents with an overview of the daily program of their child. Give them a long-range view so that they will know how you would like their child to be functioning (in academics as well as behavior) by the end of the school year.

Summarize the salient points of the conference as it draws to a close. Ask the parents if they have questions. Maintain a record of the conference, who attended, and any decisions reached.

Suggested Readings for Parents

Between Parent and Child and Between Parent and Teenager, by Haim G. Ginott (New York: Macmillan, 1969).

Dibs: In Search of Self, by Virginia M. Axline (New York: Ballantine Books, Inc., 1967).

Helping Your Child Develop His Potentialities, by Ruth Strang (New York: E.P. Dutton, 1965; paperback, New York: Award Books, 1970).

I'm OK: You're OK, by Tom Harris (New York: Harper and Row, 1970). A primer on transactional analysis.

Living with Children: New Methods for Parents and Teachers, by G. Patterson and Elizabeth Gallion (Research Press, 2612 North Mattis Ave., Champaign, Ill. 61820). A positive approach using behavior modification methods.

Parent Effectiveness Training, by Tom Gordon (New York: Peter H. Wyder, Publisher, 1970); and *Teacher Effectiveness Training* (New York: Peter H. Wyder, Publisher, 1974).

Peoplemaking (because you want to be a better parent), by Virginia Satin (Palo Alto, California: Science and Behavior Books, 1972).

AFFECTIVE-EDUCATION PROGRAMS

In the planning of an affective-education program for the adolescent, it is important that the student be an active participant in the establishment of goals toward which the student may direct his energies.

Guidelines for Goal Setting with the LD Adolescent

1. Explore with the student goals toward which he and you as his teacher agree to work.
2. Select in collaboration with the student two or three goals which he agrees to adopt as future goals.
   The goals should be chosen on the following basis:
   a. The student must perceive the goal as attainable.
   b. The teacher must perceive the goal as achievable (given the student's strengths and weaknesses).
   c. The student must have an interest in the goal.
   d. The goal should be one that is measurable.
3. Design a plan of action with the adolescent.
   a. The plan should incorporate the permission of any other person involved in the plan.
   b. It should specify behaviors and responsibilities of the student and the facilitative teacher.

4. Establish short term objectives which provide guides to the student toward the goal.
5. Indicate time lines for progress reviews on the goals.
6. Provide feedback to the student in the review sessions.
7. Adjust the goals accordingly.

Guidelines for Developing Social Awareness and Positive Self-Esteem in Students

In order for an LD adolescent to experience success as a student, it is frequently the teacher's responsibility to engineer the environment so this may occur. Students whose educational histories are fraught with learning difficulties as a result of a disability perceive themselves as "inadequate" or "deficient" when compared with their peers.

Teacher Activities to Develop Student Self-Esteem

- One of the most important responsibilities a teacher has in relation to the disabled adolescent is to be candid with him. Attempt to understand what the student *may* be experiencing without judging the student or his "feelings."

- If you feel that the seriousness or severity of the issue is beyond your ability to handle, the best service you can provide the student is to refer him to someone who is more highly trained to deal with emotional and/or social problems.

- Attempt to discuss problems with the students in candid terms—providing suggestions when you deem them appropriate. Do not suggest that the problem is "only a stage" or "it will pass" or "it's not really important."

- Remember you are there to work *with* the student. To be effective, you must communicate clearly and objectively.

Daily In-Class Journal

This is an activity that assists the student to consciously reflect on his emotional state. It is to be used as a daily class assignment for ten minutes each period, and as a supplement to other writing assignments.

For one month, the student is asked to keep a daily in-class journal to express his thoughts, feelings, and opinions. All comments are confidential and acceptable.

At the end of the month, the teacher reads the journals, and any student may request extra credit for keeping the journal.

Personal Time Line

This activity is adapted from *The Handbook for the Human Relations Approach*to Teaching* (Buffalo Public Schools).

The time line can serve as a preliminary outline to an autobiography. The teacher should initiate the activity through a discussion of the student's life experiences. The student is asked to recall events that influenced his life. These incidents should be limited to those that the student can associate with a particular feeling or attitude. These events are recorded along either side of a line. Upon completion of the time line, the student may add it to his journal.

Success Symbols

This activity is adapted from Otto (1967).* *

Have each student bring to class five objects that represent to him some success that he's had. The student then selects one of the objects and is instructed to share with the class the feelings and meaning he associates with the object.

A variation on this activity is to have the student list five success symbols he has not yet acquired, but wants to acquire someday.

The teacher must be open to the student's symbols and avoid making judgments.

The Affective Learning Activity Packet

One effective approach in affective education is to allow the student to explore independently some emotionally charged areas—ego, status, self-worth, etc. Use a Learning Activity Packet (LAP), as in Exhibit 6-2.

Source: Human Relations Education Center. James Foley, Director. Buffalo Public Schools. Used with permission of James J. Foley, Editor of The Handbook for the Human Relations Approach to Teaching.

---

* *Reprinted by permission of Charles Scribner's Sons Publishers from *A Guide to Developing Your Potential* by Herbert Otto. Copyright © 1967.

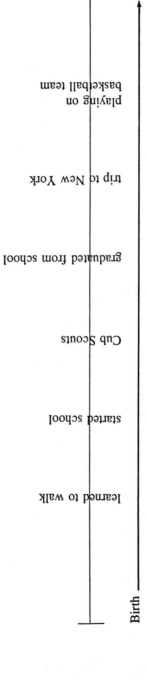

Example:

Present

playing on
basketball team

trip to New York

graduated from school

Cub Scouts

started school

learned to walk

Birth

Exhibit 6-2 Understanding Yourself Better

A Learning Activity Packet

Purpose: This packet is designed to help you understand yourself better. One way to reach this goal is to help you discover what kind of personality you have and what this means in relation to career thoughts. Your personality is the sum of all your qualities, and is different from every other person's. Your personality is made up of what you believe in and how you act toward others.

Activity: Please answer "yes" or "no" to each of the statements below. Remember this activity is to help you. It is important that you be honest in your responses.

About me   Yes   No
    1. I like working with people most of the time.
    2. I am usually outgoing.
    3. I like listening better than talking.
    4. I usually lead the conversation.
    5. I enjoy making people laugh.

About the work environment
    6. I like working outdoors.
    7. I like to be mobile.
    8. I like working at a desk.
    9. I like situations that allow me to help others.
    10. I like a setting that permits me to use questioning.

About the work task
    11. I enjoy doing highly detailed work.
    12. I like opportunities that allow me to use my powers of persuasion.
    13. I like a situation that challenges me.
    14. I like a situation that is consistent.
    15. I like variety in the work.

Exhibit 6-2 continued

Evaluating Results: If you answered "yes" to #1 and #9, you might consider becoming a nurse, doctor, social worker, hospital attendant, police officer, or personnel worker. You are a "helper."
- #3, #8, you might consider becoming a librarian, journalist, or editor. You are a "listener."
- #2, #12, you might consider becoming a salesperson or lawyer. You are a "persuader."
- #6, you might consider becoming a farmer, ranger, or telephone lineman. You are an "outdoor person."
- #10, #13, you might consider becoming a chemist, biologist, or lab technician. You are a "questioner."
- #11, you might consider becoming a bookkeeper, accountant, secretary, or typist. You are a "detailer."

Think about the remaining statements as they apply to you. These listed occupations are not all inclusive (e.g., there are many other potential jobs for an outdoor person). The occupations that are listed do not match up perfectly with the personality types under which they are listed. This LAP is to assist you in looking at yourself in relation to career choices.

Understanding yourself means knowing your interests. The more interests you have the better chance you have of finding a career that will satisfy you.

Activities
1. Think about the different roles you play each day (such as family member, student, friend, team member). Act out some of these roles in class, showing how your behavior differs in each role.
2. Pick a good friend from among your classmates. List the personality traits that you believe describe what your friend is really like. Then switch roles. Compare your lists and write a paragraph about how personality traits combine to make each person unique.
3. Check the "Help Wanted" sections of local newspapers for ads that interest you. Write "make believe" responses to these ads, listing abilities you have that might qualify you for those jobs.

With a Little Help from Your Friends*

Schrank (1972) suggests this activity.

The group members sit in a circle. One person volunteers to go first. The others in the group take turns giving honest compliments to the volunteer. The person receiving compliments may not make any reply to the group (such as saying "Thank you"). Each person in the group takes a turn receiving compliments from the others. A group member may pass when it is his turn to be the compliment-receiver, but not when he is to be the compliment-giver. Everyone has to think of one honestly positive thing to say to everyone else.

After the activity, the group should talk about the feelings they had during the session, especially when receiving compliments; e.g., "Why do we feel embarrassed when praised, even if we know that the compliment is true?"

For a variation on this activity, divide the class into groups to give and receive compliments, then hold the discussion as a class.

Telegrams**

Simon et al. (1972) suggest this activity.

Students are asked to compose telegrams that contain important messages that they wish they could send to people they know. Each telegram must begin "Dear _____ ." The body of each telegram must start with "I urge you to . . . ," "I wish you would . . . ," or "I want you to. . . ." Each message must contain 25 words or less; the fewer words, the better. The author must sign his name.

After everyone has written a telegram, each person reads his telegram aloud, including his own name at the end. However, the author need not reveal to the rest of the group the intended recipient of the telegram if he doesn't wish to do so. (When it is time to read the telegram, he may simply omit reading the "Dear _____ .")

The purpose of this activity is to help the student say what he really wants to say to people and to force him to be responsible for what he says (thus, the insistence that he sign and read his own name). Within the time available, the leader may ask each student to send a telegram to his mother, father, teacher, best friend, principal, and classmate of his choice, etc.

You will find that for the first few rounds students tend to be silly and superficial, but that by the end of the exercise they are really saying what they want to say to people.

---

*Reprinted by permission of Beacon Press from *Teaching Human Beings: 101 Subversive Activities for the Classroom,* by Jeffrey Schrank. Copyright © 1972.

**Reprinted by permission of A & W Publishers, Inc. from *Values Clarification: A Handbook of Practical Strategies for Teachers and Students,* by Sidney B. Simon, Leland W. Howe, and Howard Kirschenbaum. Copyright © 1972; Copyright © 1978 by Hart Publishing Company, Inc.

The point to be brought out in discussion is that we are often not honest about our wishes or our feelings, especially if we are sending a message that the recipient might interpret as negative. A vehicle such as this makes it easier for us to crystallize thoughts and feelings. "What are the problems that this class has that make teachers say it's the 'worst class'?"

Discussion Questions

Discussion questions can be used to fill in time after any of the other activities, or as an activity in themselves. After the leader puts out a few ideas for discussion and leads the conversation, the students should be asked to throw out some topics that they would like to talk about. Good discussion questions include:

- Do you think children should work for an allowance?
- Do you think there are times when cheating is O.K.?
- Do you enjoy doing things with your family?
- Would you like to be cremated after you die?
- What do you think about seat belts?
- Do you feel closer to one of your parents than the other?
- Would you dye your hair?
- What do you think of mercy killing?
- What do you think of capital punishment?
- Have you ever seen a dead body?
- Do you think you are a failure?
- What would you like to be doing right now?
- Do you like beards?
- Are you hurt when you're criticized?
- Are you willing to admit when you're wrong?
- Would you give money to a beggar on the street?
- Do you have difficulty sitting still?
- Would you donate your body to science when you die?

Preferred Qualities in Students

In designing a program of affective education, the teacher must be aware of the qualities in students that influence how he regards his students. A vehicle that may be used to compare how educators who work together rank-order student qualities is suggested in Exhibit 6-3, which is adapted from Hurley and Randolph (1971).

Affective Education: Therapeutic Approaches

The teacher must attempt to understand the student's affective dynamics through decoding, labeling and redirection behaviors (Long, Alpher, Butt & Cally, 1976). Decoding is a process that enables a teacher to obtain clues to a student's inner life through the student's verbal and nonverbal communications. Through labeling, the teacher verbalizes what he "thinks" a child may be feeling (e.g., "It seems to me that you are angry."). The next step is to accept the student's *feelings*, although this does *not* require that the teacher also accept the student's *behavior*. (The distinction between feelings and behavior is critical.) In redirection, appropriate behaviors for expressing feelings are sought.

Therapeutic approaches that are relevant to the educational system and the education of the total child include:

- the psychoeducational model
- the conflict model
- reality therapy
- Adlerian psychology
- life-space interviewing
- behavior modification

It is important that every teacher become conversant with the distinguishing characteristics and advantages of each approach.

The Psychoeducational Model

The psychoeducational model postulates a circular interaction between thoughts and feelings; i.e., cognitive experience affects emotional experience, and vice versa. Thus, the child with great reading difficulty might develop intensely adverse emotional reactions to his failure, while the child with severe anxiety over performance might experience great difficulty learning to read. This model is particularly relevant to the LD adolescent whose academic failure or frustration results in a concomitant emotional problem.

Exhibit 6-3 A Rank-Order of Student Qualities

Instructions After reading through the qualities or characteristics of children listed below, assign the number "1" to the quality that you believe to be the most desirable quality for a ___-year-old. Assign number "2" to the attribute you regard as second in importance, and so on until you have assigned a number to all ten of the qualities listed. You may, of course, change your mind or correct any assigned numbers as you go along. Assign a number to each of these ten attributes, even if you find it difficult to make some choices. No tie scores, please.

Preferred Qualities of Children

Boy		Girl
	A. responsible and trustworthy	
	B. neat and clean	
	C. curious	
	D. interacts well with others	
	E. considerate and cooperative	
	F. assertive and self-reliant	
	G. able to make friends	
	H. respectful toward adults	
	I. fun-loving and carefree	
	J. imaginative and carefree	

Scoring:
When each member of the team has completed the form, team members should compare their answers freely. The leader should instruct each participant to add his scores for C, F, and J (understructured characteristics), and compare that total with the total of B, E, and H (structured qualities). There are no "right" answers, but the different values of team members become apparent.

Source: Reprinted from "Preferred Qualities of Children Activity," by John R. Hurley, 1971 with permission.

These are the conceptual attributes of a psychoeducational approach as derived from Fagan, Long, and Stevens (1975).

1. It is assumed that cognitive and affective processes are in constant interaction.
2. To understand behavior means to understand relevant phenomenal aspects of a child's life-space.
3. Behavior consists of both the verbal and nonverbal expressions of a total functioning person. It is the person, not the expression, that is the most important consideration.
4. Behavior becomes a matter for concern when it perpetrates personal unhappiness, self-deprecation, or conflict, or when it creates serious disturbance with existing social norms.
5. To understand behavior, an individual must be aware of the cognitive, affective, and motivational processes in oneself and others.
6. Understanding behavior is achieved by assessing and communicating with and about the learner and significant others in his life-space.
7. The task of modifying behaviors which are deemed self-defeating involves a process of establishing objectives that are determined in relation to total personal functioning.
8. Understanding a student's behavior enables the teacher to create conditions that facilitate behavioral improvement.
9. The measure of personal growth on the part of the student is the extent to which personal behavior derives from self-control rather than external control.
10. Emotions are significant personal events. They are to be understood, accepted, and valued.
11. Learning involves increasing understanding of and satisfaction with things, symbols, oneself, and others.

The Conflict Model

Three major proponents of this model (Long, Morse and Newman, 1976) were influenced by Redl and Wineman (1957). Long, who developed the conflict model, views the environment as an essential factor in deviant behavior. His model, paraphrased, argues that:

1. A child in conflict views the classroom through eyes colored by his unique life history.
2. A child in conflict is one who is vulnerable to specific school-related tasks (i.e., competition, separation, etc.).

3. Positive and negative feelings within and between children are normal, healthy and necessary to a fulfilling life.
4. Each child has been socialized to process his feelings through direct expression, using coping techniques and defense mechanisms.
5. Under severe stress a child's behavior is observed to regress. The progress is from coping techniques to defense techniques then to primitive expression of feelings.
6. The problem behavior of a child in conflict represents his present solution to stress.

Reality Therapy

Glasser (1965) developed an approach predicated upon the tenet that there are two needs each individual seeks to satisfy in life. They are: (1) the need to love and be loved, and (2) the need to feel worthwhile to ourselves and others.

LD adolescents have been precluded from feeling worthwhile in school because of their learning problems. The primary task of the teacher, according to Glasser, is to teach the LD student to become more self-responsible. This is accomplished when the teacher adheres to the following principles:

1. Each student should be treated as a complex human being.
2. The student should be viewed as being responsible for his own behavior.
3. The teacher should deal with the student in the present tense.

Natural consequences are those events that occur without having been arranged by the teacher; logical consequences are structured and arranged by the teacher. One advantage of using consequences instead of punishment to change behavior is that the teacher can avoid struggles over authority with the adolescent. Furthermore, the student can choose the manner in which he will respond. The student is encouraged to persevere toward his goal of behavior change.

The efficacy of this approach in modifying the behavior of the LD adolescent is difficult to substantiate empirically because its practitioners tend to publish case-study and anecdotal reports rather than experimental vs. control group comparisons.

Life-Space Interviewing

This approach has direct relevance to the LD adolescent, whose educational life is commonly fraught with crises.

There are two basic goals inherent in this method: (1) clinical exploitation of life events, and (2) the provision of emotional first aid to the student at his moment of crisis. A basic tenet is that intervention at critical times enhances the student's receptivity to assistance.

The suggested procedure for the teacher is adapted from Morse (1976):

1. In a nonjudgmental way, explore the student's perception of what has happened.
2. Ascertain the significance the student ascribes to the incident.
3. Help the student recreate the situation, based on his perceptions.
4. Convey empathy for the student's feelings.
5. Refrain from value judgments through word or behavior.
6. Explain areas of possible "change."
7. Develop and present to the student a plan for constructive future action.

This approach offers the teacher a number of advantages:

- It is insight-producing, and produces a plan for future behavior.

- It focuses on behavioral or attitudinal change.

- It has promise for long-term behavioral improvement.

- It helps the student become responsible for his own behavior.

Behavior Modification

Certain behaviors common among LD adolescents interfere with educational potential. Among the more prevalent are (1) inadequate self-control, and (2) academic and social frustration.

Inadequate Self-Control: The student who has difficulty sticking with a task may be assisted by a teacher who:

- *Provides cues and promptings.* This behavior is part of every teacher's repertoire, and includes tapping, signaling, and similar tactics designed to bring the student back to the task at hand.

- *Reinforces on-task behavior.* The teacher should convey interest in, and reinforcement for, completed work.

- *Ignores off-task behavior.* While reinforcing the student's on-task behavior, the teacher should ignore the student who is demonstrating off-task behavior.

- *Controls the student's behavior through physical proximity.* Moving close to the student in a low-key manner has the effect of enhancing the student's attending behavior.

These suggestions are offered as viable responses to the student whose behavior is generally appropriate, and who can often regain control independent of adult influence. The strategies may be categorized as preventive measures, in that they can reduce the likelihood that more severe incidents will occur.

Academic and Social Frustration: The LD student with a long history of academic difficulty frequently finds himself in stressful situations. The teacher who observes this stress should:

- *Offer skill assistance.* The teacher ignores the inappropriate behavior the student is manifesting in response to his frustration. The teacher focuses his attention on the specific academic skill or issue that is responsible for creating the student's frustration. He offers to assist the student.

- *Redesign the classroom environment.* The key factor in a teacher's ability to lessen a student's academic or social frustration is his sensitivity to the student's dynamic state. Suggest, for example, an in-seat supplementary activity for a group of students who appear "hyper," or an action-oriented lesson for a lethargic group.

- *"Clean" the setting.* This is a preventive measure wherein the teacher removes from the student objects that the teacher believes would tempt the student away from his work.

- *Use an appeal approach.* The effectiveness of this approach depends on the teacher's accuracy in knowing what the student values in his life. The teacher then attempts to "reach" the student through appealing to the student's own value system. If the student values the esteem of his peers, for example, the teacher would employ peer pressure or peer modeling.

Guidelines for Managing a Classroom

In addition to dealing with specific problems of individual students, the teacher should organize his classroom in line with some basic techniques that have proven successful in motivating students to pursue positive, constructive goals. The techniques are called "behavior modification" or "contingency contracting." Many of the basic principles are summed up by "Grandma's Law," which says: "First clean up your plate. Then you may have dessert."

Homme (1970) suggests contingency contracting with the adolescent student. A "contingency contract" is an agreement between student and teacher that defines what consequences can be expected to follow a desired behavior. It details both the teacher's and the student's expectations. The ten rules of contingency contracting, adapted from Homme, are:

1. Rewards should be immediate. Initial contracts should call for small bits of desired behavior.
2. Initial contracts should call for and reward small approximations; i.e., small, simple-to-perform behaviors that approximate the ultimately desired performance. For example, initially require and reward the completion of two problems, rather than the completion of an entire lesson.
3. Give small, frequent rewards. Many small reinforcements are more effective than a few large ones.
4. Call for and reward accomplishment rather than obedience. Emphasis should be on "If you accomplish," rather than "If you do as I say."
5. Reward performance after it occurs. The "first work and then play" sequence must be applied systematically and consistently. Never reverse the order.
6. The contract must be fair. The amount of the reward should fairly reflect the amount of performance required.
7. The terms of the contract must be positive. The contract should contribute to the child's performance and experience, not take something away from him. It should not threaten punishment.
8. The terms of the contract must be clear. The student must know how much is expected of him, and what he can expect as a result of his performance.
9. The contract must be honest. Carry out the contract immediately and in accordance with specific terms.
10. Contracting as a method must be used systematically. Once contracting has been established as a mode of motivation, it should be maintained—making sure that undesirable behavior is never rewarded in any way.

The Need for Introspection

A teacher should routinely use introspection as an integral facet of teaching. This helps to keep him on track. See Exhibit 6-4 for a guide to effective introspection.

Exhibit 6-4 Introspection Guide for Teachers

---

1. Look at yourself in relation to your student's behavior.
2. Look at the behavior of your student as a function of the learning environment you create.
3. Consider the following questions:
   a. Am I providing sound remediation in the necessary area?
   b. Have I built in motivation, incentive, and reward?
   c. Have I provided necessary structure?
   d. Am I fostering personal success and independent performance?
4. Accept the reality of your role as a remediation agent. Reflect on the following thoughts:

   The remedial teacher must be resourceful. If, after a fair attempt to utilize one method, the pupil has not made adequate progress, the teacher must be willing to try something else. Adaptability to the pupil's needs is far more important than devotion to a particular plan or procedure (Harris, 1970, p. 363).

   There is no one single etiology for all learning disabilities. Rather, learning problems can be caused by any number of a multiplicity of factors, all of which may be highly interrelated. Unfortunately, all too often the child who is experiencing a learning disorder is approached with a unitary orientation so that extremely important aspects of his unique learning problems may well be ignored. The tendency of each professional discipline to view the entire problem "through its own window of specialization" often obscures vital factors which may contribute to, or at least exacerbate, the basic difficulty. It is just as involved to conceive of one cure, one panacea, applied randomly to all types of learning disorders. Not every learning disabled youngster requires a special school, or psychotherapy, or kinesthetic techniques, or perceptual-motor training, or, for that matter, to regress to crawling along the floor! (Abrams, 1970, p. 299)

HOW TO INTRODUCE YOUR CLASS TO THE MAINSTREAMED STUDENT

Preparing regular education students to receive exceptional classmates is an important—though commonly neglected—aspect of the mainstreaming process. Regular classes might routinely be exposed to some of the materials below.

The Summer of the Swans, by Betsy Byars. From Viking Press, 625 Madison Avenue, New York, NY 10022. $5.95. Also, in paperback, from Avon Books, 959 Eighth Avenue, New York, NY 10019. $1.25. This book focuses on an adolescent girl and her 14th summer. She is moody, unpredictable, and does not understand herself. The central episode revolves around her mentally retarded younger brother, who is mute (grades 6-8).

Joyride, by Betty Cavanna. From William Morrow & Co., Inc., 105 Madison Avenue, New York, NY 10016. $6.95. This story about a high-school girl lame from polio is set in a small town in the 1920s. She learns that she can compete on equal terms with her peers (grades 7-8).

On the Move, by Harriet M. Savitz. From Harper & Row, Inc., 10 East 53rd Street, New York, NY 10022. $5.95. The story concerns a rehabilitation center for young paraplegics (grades 6-8).

The Witch's Brat, by Rosemary Sutcliff. From Henry Z. Walch, Inc., 750 Third Avenue, New York, NY 10017. $6.50. This stirring novel is about a crippled boy who becomes a healer and helps others in 12th-century England (grades 7-8).

Your Handicap: Don't Let It Handicap You, by Sarah Splaver. From Julian Messner, 1230 Avenue of the Americas, New York, NY 10020. For the handicapped child this book offers encouragement, role models, a positive path from disabilities to abilities, and career and college information. Handicapped and nonhandicapped children alike can benefit from the discussions of blindness, deafness, orthopedic problems and appliances, diabetes, and epilepsy (grades 6-8).

Kelly's Creek, by Doris B. Smith. From Thomas Y. Crowell Co., 521 Fifth Ave., New York, NY 10017. $6.95. This is the story of a learning-disabled nine-year-old who is misunderstood by his parents, classmates, and teachers (grades 8 and up).

Self-Concept Bibliography

Awareness, by John P. Stevens (Real People Press, Box F, Moab, UT 84532, 1971, 275 pgs. 1973, 309 pgs.). This book includes 100 exercises drawn from Gestalt awareness training activities. It includes personal awareness, communication, exercises using art, movement, and sound.

Encounter with the Self, by Donald E. Hamachek (New York: Holt, Rinehart and Winston, 1971, 264 pgs.). Written for educators. Includes case histories, anecdotal materials, and current research.

Perceiving, Behaving, and Becoming, ed. by Arthur W. Combs (Yearbook of the Association for Supervision and Curriculum Development, 1701 K Street, N.W., Washington, DC 20006, 1962). This book contains a series of articles by leading educational theorists in perception, self-concept, and self-actualization.

Psycho-Cybernetics, by Maxwell Maltz (Englewood Cliffs, NJ: Prentice-Hall, 1960). Using real-life examples, the author shows how one can create a totally new image of oneself as a successful and happy person. The use of creative imagery is a very important part of self-concept improvement. Maltz offers many suggestions.

Psychosynthesis: A Manual of Principles and Techniques, by Roberto Assagioli (New York: Hobbs, Dorman and Co., 1965; paperback, New York: Viking Press, 1970). Psychosynthesis is a way of pulling together all of the various trends in humanistic psychology and education. It is an approach that fosters the balanced development of the body, feelings, mind, and spirit around a unifying center of being and awareness—"The Transpersonal Self." Assagioli's work on the "Ideal Self" is very helpful in self-concept work.

Pygmalion in the Classroom: Teacher's Expectations and Pupil's Intellectual Development, by Robert Rosenthal and L. Jacobsen (New York: Holt, Rinehart and Winston, 1968). Rosenthal and Jacobsen report their research, indicating that whatever a teacher expects from a student he will probably get. The need for the teacher to "believe in" the child's ability to succeed is amply supported by their work.

Schools Without Failure, by William Glasser (New York: Harper & Row Pubs., Inc. 1969, 235 pgs.). Glasser offers a new approach to reduce school failures—an approach based on personal involvement, relevance, and thinking—and demonstrates how to help negatively-oriented students aim for positive goal setting, personal achievement and individual responsibility.

Teacher and Child, by Haim G. Ginott (New York: Macmillan, 1972, 323 pgs.). Ginott goes beyond mere theory and offers teachers a model for a language of acceptance and compassion. His suggestions are designed to increase a child's sense of self-worth and to enhance the quality of life in the classroom.

The Antecedents of Self-Esteem, by Stanley Coopersmith (San Francisco: W.H. Freeman & Co., 1967). This is a doctoral dissertation on the self-esteem of a group of junior-high boys.

Values Clarification: A Handbook of Practical Strategies for Teachers and Students, by Sidney B. Simon, Leland W. Howe, and Howard Kirschenbaum (New York: Hart Publishing Co., 1972, 397 pgs.). This book contains 79 classroom exercises designed to help students clarify their values.

REFERENCES

Fagan, S.A., Long, N.J., and Stevens, D.J. *Teaching children self-control: Preventing emotional and learning problems in the elementary school.* Columbus, Ohio: Charles E. Merrill Publishing Co., 1975.

Glasser, W. *Reality therapy: A new approach to psychiatry.* New York: Harper & Row, 1965.

Handbook for the Human Relations Approach to Teaching. Human Relations Education Center. James Foley, Director. Buffalo Public School, Buffalo, New York.

Harris, A.J. *How to increase reading ability.* (5th ed.). New York: David McKay Publishing Co., 1970.

Hewett, F. & Watson, P. *Teacher attitudes toward mainstreaming: A preliminary report.* University of California, Los Angeles, California, 1975.

Homme, L. *How to use contingency contracting in the classroom.* Champaign, Illinois: Research Press, 1970.

Hurley, J. & Randolph, L. "Behavior Attributes Preferred in Eight Year Olds." JSAS Journal of Selected Documents in Psychology. 1971.

Long, A.J.; Alpher, R.; Butt, F.; and Cully, M. Helping children cope with feelings. *Conflict in the classroom* 3rd ed. Edited by N. Long, W. Morse, and R. Newman. Belmont, California: Wadsworth, 1976, pp. 297-301.

Long, N.J., & Newman, R.G. Managing surface behavior of children in school. In N.J. Long, W.C. Morse, & R.G. Newman (Eds.), *Conflict in the classroom* (3rd ed.). Belmont, California: Wadsworth, 1976.

Morse, W. The crisis or helping teacher. In N.J. Long, W.C. Morse, & R.G. Newman (Eds.), *Conflict in the classroom* (3rd ed.). Belmont, California: Wadsworth, 1976.

Otto, H. *A guide to developing your potential.* New York: Charles Scribner's Sons, 1967.

Redl, F., & Wineman, D. *The aggressive child.* Glencoe, Illinois: The Free Press, 1957.

Schrank, J. *Teaching human beings: 101 subversive activities for the classroom.* Boston: Beacon Press, 1972.

Simon, S.G., Howe, L.W., and Kirschenbaum, H. *Values clarification: A handbook of practical strategies for teachers and students.* New York: Hart Publishing Co., 1972.

Tornquist, L. *Group work model activities.* Center for Applied Instruction, Southwest Minnesota College, 1971.

SUGGESTED READINGS

Abrams, J.C. Learning disabilities: A complex phenomenon. *The Reading Teacher*. January 1970, 229-303.

Alley, G. & Deshler, D. *Teaching the LD Adolescent: Strategies and Methods.* Denver: Love Publishing Co., 1979.

Dreikus, R., & Sonstegard, M. Rationale of group counseling. *Guidance and counseling in the elementary school: Reading in theory and practice.* (ed. Don C. Dinkmeyer) New York: Holt, Rinehart and Winston, Inc., 1968.

Edwards, G. *Reaching Out*. Garden City, New Jersey: Ideal Publishing Co., Inc., 1972.

Koch, K. *Wishes, lies, dreams*. New York: Random House, 1971.

Long, N.J. "Nicholas J. Long" *Teaching Children with Behavior Disorders: Personal Perspectives*. Edited by M.J. Kauffman and C.D. Lewis. Columbus: C.E. Merrill, 1974.

Sutton, T. *Looking, feeling, seeing, growing. A program of feeling activities for the classroom*. Orono, Maine: University of Maine, Orono Press.

Chapter 7

Programming for LD
Adolescents: A Perspective

7

In 1966, Congress created the Bureau of Education for the Handicapped. In 1970, the first "Education of the Handicapped Children Act" became law. In 1971, Congress amended the Act to expand the federal role in its administration (P.L. 93-380). Most recently, further amendments emerged as the "Education for All Handicapped Children Act," (P.L. 94-142).

The educational problems of the handicapped are many and varied, as stated in Section 3 of P.L. 94-142:

> There are more than eight million handicapped children in the United States; one million are excluded entirely from education; more than half of the handicapped children are receiving inappropriate services; families are forced to find services at great distance from their homes and at great expense.

Another Act, enacted in 1973, further strengthened the rights of handicapped students to an appropriate education. Section 504 of this Act, the "Rehabilitation Act" (P.L. 93-112), established that the educational rights of the handicapped are federal civil rights. HEW's Office of Civil Rights (OCR) was designated to protect these statutory rights.

Together, these statutes clearly dictate that handicapped students be identified, evaluated, and appropriately placed.

P.L. 94-142 mandates that special education students be offered programs in the least restrictive setting. This means that the LD student must enter the educational mainstream whenever that is feasible.

147

MAINSTREAM PLANNING

There are both pros and cons associated with the concept of integrating special students within regular classes. Grotsky (1976) identified several considerations that fall into each category. A discussion of the advantages and disadvantages of mainstream placement of LD students follows.

Advantages

1. Mainstreaming is perceived of as normalization as children normally attend general education programs.
2. Exceptional children have been shown to exhibit academic progress in regular class settings provided that adequate instructional services and modifications are made to accommodate their special learning needs.
3. The changing role of the resource LD teacher provides the mainstream teacher with support in the planning of a program for the integrated student.
4. The attenuation of the stigma of being "exceptional" for the adolescent significantly improves his interest in school and his academic motivation.
5. The flexibility and options available within the regular class setting enables the teacher to employ a variety of innovative approaches for improved learning environments. Some of these include: nongraded classes, the open classroom and individualized prescribed instruction.

Disadvantages

1. Many regular classroom teachers lack the competencies necessary to effectively mainstream exceptional children.
2. The teacher's feelings of inadequacy with the mainstream student may result in a classroom climate that is tense and counterproductive to learning.
3. The mandates for resources assured under P.L. 94-142 may not be available in regular programs.
4. The mainstream setting may not allow for the degree of parental involvement that is essential to the maintenance of the exceptional student in the mainstream.
5. Students who feel inadequate as a result of a learning disability may, through peer comparison in the integrated class, have these feelings further exacerbated.
6. If there is not both administrative and teacher support for mainstreaming, the effectiveness of the activity is limited.

SOME PRINCIPLES OF LEARNING

Whatever the specific educational setting (mainstream or other type of place-ment) deemed most appropriate for the LD adolescent, there are certain universal principles of learning that should be followed.

Learning is most effective when:

- the learning objectives and philosophy of the program are planned and clearly understood by both the teacher and the student;
- reciprocal respect and a friendly atmosphere exist between the teacher and the learner;
- the student has meaningful, satisfying, and realistic goals that guide his learning activities;
- motivation is provided through a regard for the needs, interests, problems, and concerns of the learner;
- an attractive, safe, and healthful learning environment is provided;
- the learner is carefully studied by the teacher, and provision is made for his individuality;
- the learning activities and experiences are supplemented and enriched by the use of related materials;
- a tolerance for failure is developed through the provision of a backlog of successes;
- the learner engages in active, real-life experiences that are related to one another and to the problems of home, school, and community; and
- there is continuous and periodic evaluation of the student and the program.

THE THREE INGREDIENTS OF LEARNING

Irrespective of the subject matter or the specific instructional approach, three specific things must occur before learning can take place:

1. A source of information must be available to the potential learner (e.g., a book, material, machine, lecture, etc.).
2. The learner must respond to the information presented.
3. Frequent and well-informed evaluations and diagnoses must be carefully integrated with the learning experience to enable the determination of the most appropriate educational decisions.

BASIC CLASSROOM CONSIDERATIONS

In the learning process, the teacher is the catalyst: he can significantly affect the student's potential for learning by manipulating the learning environment.

Factors that affect student learning were succinctly stated by Sartor (1956). She presented these considerations as questions the teacher may use as an introspective guide.

How Good a Teacher Am I? *

1. Do I make my assignments clear and specific so that each pupil knows what is expected of them?
2. Do I provide for individual differences in the classroom?
3. Do I encourage my pupils to work rather than drive them?
4. Do I teach with the knowledge at my command, yet avoid acting like a know-it-all?
5. Do I recognize the worth of each individual and encourage creativeness rather than expect students to conform to a pattern?
6. Do I use frequent evaluations to check pupil accomplishments?
7. Do I make good use of available teaching materials and watch for new materials as they are developed?

CRITERIA FOR AN IDEAL CURRICULUM

The teacher's responsibility is to define a curriculum that is both appropriate and relevant.

A curriculum should be designed so that the inherent objectives correlate with the student's needs (as he perceives them) and his developmental stage.

The criteria for an ideal curriculum include:

- a clear statement of assumptions about the learner, incorporating his educational needs, strengths, and weaknesses;

- a clear statement of objectives (i.e., what the learner should be able to do as a result of the educational experience or activity);

- a clear statement of the teacher's and student's performance expectations in the learning situation; and

- a feedback mechanism to the student regarding his performance.

*Reprinted from "How Good a Teacher Am I?" *NEA Journal,* October 1956, *45,* 448, by permission of publisher and the author, Lina Sartor.

Additional considerations include alternative ways for the student to demonstrate his knowledge. These should be individualized, reflecting the specific disability of the adolescent.

An ideal curriculum for the LD adolescent is student-focused. This is contrary to the average secondary-level curriculum, which is subject-focused. Focusing on the student gives the curriculum an inherent integration.

INTEGRATING REMEDIATION AND COMPENSATION FOR THE ADOLESCENT

The secondary-level teacher must consider many factors relating to the LD adolescent when he is designing a curriculum. Whether to continue remediating the adolescent's learning disability—or to teach the student compensation techniques—is a prime consideration.

In developing an instructional curriculum for the LD adolescent, the teacher must consider both remediation and compensation. Remedial instruction directly addresses the student's specific disabilities; compensatory teaching focuses on using the student's abilities as a means of mastering subject matter content.

There is no research that definitively establishes the superiority of either approach. It seems logical, however, to advocate an integrated program combining the two approaches. If instruction does not take the child's disability into account, he will be unable to master the content presented. Conversely, if the sole emphasis is on ameliorating the disability, the student's concept acquisition will not keep pace with his peers'.

Remediation Techniques

Specific strategies teachers use in addressing the LD adolescent's learning problems should derive from an analysis of the variables in the learning situation, the subject matter to be learned, the environment in which the learning is to occur, and from the learner himself.

The learner. The teacher should assess the student's processing modes (auditory, visual, tactile), memory, and language abilities. The educational plan designed for the student should incorporate processing instruction (derived from the analysis) into the academic skill instructional plan.

Strategies may be selected as a function of the student's test performance. Here a particular test is used to identify the specific areas in need of remediation.

Remediation needs may be determined, also, using the hierarchical stages of development of a normal child as a reference. Remedial efforts would be geared toward assisting the student to complete growth at an "unfinished stage" and proceed to the next stage of development.

The subject. Remedial efforts here suggest the use of specialized materials and techniques and identification of the level of skill development in the sequential hierarchy of skills inherent in a given task. The teacher's remedial focus is on the task to be learned.

The environment. Remediation may involve attempting to change the student's behavior by establishing specific desirable behavior in the student's repertoire. Consideration is given to the manner in which environmental conditions affect the student's academic and affective behavior.

Compensation Techniques in the Mainstream Class

For the student who experiences severe reading difficulty, prerecord lessons and allow the student to use earphones as he reads. This technique provides the student both visual and auditory input.

For the student who can comprehend the steps in a mathematical process—but cannot perform the basic computations—provide a pocket calculator.

For the student who cannot contend with multiple ideas at one time, provide a sheet containing the major concepts. Such a sheet is also an excellent guide for the student to employ in preparing for tests.

Encourage the student whose reading difficulties are exacerbated by regressive eye movements to use his finger to track the printed words across the page.

Allow the student to compensate for his learning difficulty by giving him extra time to process information.

INDIVIDUALIZED EDUCATION PROGRAM

Whether you emphasize compensation or remediation, the educational plan for the student should be developed through a collaborative, team approach. The product of the team's effort is an Individualized Education Program (IEP).

Once a child is evaluated, and identified as "exceptional," an IEP is developed. P.L. 94-142 mandates that each special-education student have an IEP. Furthermore, the law clearly states what this plan must include. It is important that all educators become conversant with the necessary IEP components, as the responsibility in large degree resides with the mainstream teachers. IEP requirements are outlined in Exhibit 7-1.

Exhibit 7-1 IEP Components

Present Level of Functioning: This is to include the full range of problems that might need to be addressed in a program of special education and related services.

Annual Goals: The plan must include a statement of reasonable progress expectations.

Related Services: In addition to basic instructional services, the plan should include any supportive services the child may require.

Regular Education Participation: The plan should reflect the degree to which the child can participate in "mainstream" education.

Time Constraints: Dates when services are to be initiated and concluded must be indicated.

Accountability: The plan must state evaluation procedures and schedules to measure the appropriateness and effectiveness of the short-term objectives.

Source: The Education for All Handicapped Children Act (P.L. 94-142), 1975.

The LD Adolescent and P.L. 94-142

The "Education for All Handicapped Children Act," which became law in 1975, has direct relevance for the teacher who works with LD adolescents in the mainstream.

The intent of this Act is to ensure (1) that each handicapped student is offered a free, appropriate public education that includes the special-education services and related services necessary to meet the student's needs; and (2) that the rights of these students and their parents are protected under the law. A significant aspect of the mandate requires each school district to assess and ensure the effectiveness of efforts to educate those children.

Free, Appropriate Public Education

A "free, appropriate public education" refers to special-education services and related services that (a) are provided free of charge (at public expense) under public supervision and direction; (b) meet the standards of the state educational agency; (c) include preschool, elementary-school, and secondary-school education; and (d) are provided in conformity with an individualized education program.

Related Services

Such support services as transportation, corrective interventions, and remedial interventions are referred to as "related services." This category includes speech pathology and audiology, psychological services, physical and occupational therapy, early identification and assessment of a child's handicap, school social-work services, counseling services (including counseling and training parents, providing parents with information about child development, and helping parents to understand the special needs of their child), and medical services for diagnostic or evaluation purposes.

Each state and local education agency must take steps to ensure that handicapped children are offered the variety of programs and services available to nonhandicapped children, including art, music, industrial arts, home economics, vocational education, physical education, and nonacademic and extracurricular services and activities.

The Planning Conference

The determination of the most appropriate program for a handicapped student is made in a collaborative planning conference.

The local education agency must ensure that each conference to develop an IEP includes:

- a representative of the local education agency (other than the child's teacher) who is (a) in the field of school administration, supervision, or special education; and (b) meets the state's certification requirements;

- the child's teacher or teachers (special or regular); and

- one or both of the child's parents (and, where appropriate, the child).

Parent Participation

Each local education agency must take steps to ensure that one or both parents attend the planning meeting or are afforded the opportunity to participate, including scheduling the meeting at a mutually convenient time and place. If neither parent can attend, the local education agency must use other methods to ensure parent participation, such as individual or conference telephone calls. Furthermore, the local education agency must take whatever action is necessary to ensure that parents understand the proceedings; e.g., arranging for interpreters for parents who are deaf or whose native language is other than English.

PERSONNEL DEVELOPMENT

The school is responsible for developing a personnel development plan that provides for the in-service training of general- and special-education instructional and support personnel, detailed procedures to ensure that all personnel needed to carry out the purposes of the Act are appropriately and adequately prepared and trained, and effective procedures for acquiring and disseminating information to teachers and administrators of programs for handicapped children.

THE CLASSROOM TEACHERS

The regulations under P.L. 94-142 stipulate that a state's annual program plan must provide incentives to ensure participation by teachers in professional development activities. Examples of reinforcers used by some states include: payment for participants, academic credit, salary credit, and certification renewal.

REFERENCES

Grotsky, Mainstreaming, integration, deinstitutionalization, nonlabeling, normalization. In Mann (Ed.) *Shared Responsibility for Handicapped Students,* Banyan Books, Inc., Coral Gables, FL, 1976.

Sartor, L. How good a teacher am I? *NEA Journal,* October 1956, *45,* 448.

SUGGESTED READINGS

McCarthy, J. *Report of Leadership Training Institute.* Presented at ACLD, New York, February 1975.

Minskoff, J.G. Learning disabled children at the secondary level: Educational programming in perspective. J. Arena (Ed.). *The child with learning disabilities: His right to learn.* Proceedings of the Eighth Annual International Conference of the ACLD, Chicago, March, 1971.

Wiederholt, J.L. *A report on secondary school programs for the learning disabled.* Final report. (Project No. H12-7145B, Grant No. OEG-0-714425), Washington, D.C.: Bureau of Education for the Handicapped, 1975.

IEP—READINGS AND RESOURCES

Abeson, A., & Zettel, J. The end of the quiet revolution: The education for all handicapped persons act of 1975, *Exceptional Children,* October 1977, pp. 115-128.

Ballard, J., & Zettel, J. "Public law 94-142 and section 504: What they say about rights and protections," *Exceptional Children,* November 1977, pp. 117-184.

Cole, R.W., & Dunn, R. A new lease on life for education of the handicapped: Ohio copes with 94-142, *Phi Delta Kappan,* September 1977, pp. 3-22.

DeBow, S. Public law 94-142, *American Annals of the Deaf,* October 1977, pp. 468-469.

Edgar, G. Individual education plans (IEP's) for severely and profoundly handicapped students. Paper delivered at the National Topical Working Conference sponsored by the Bureau of Education for the Handicapped, August 9-11, 1977.

Fanning, P. The new relationship between parents and schools, *Focus on Exceptional Children*, October 1977, *9*(5), 1-10.

Final regs for P.L. 94-142 out, major shift in policy on IEP, *Education of the Handicapped*, August 1977, *3*(17), 1-2.

Functions of the Placement Committee in Special Education: A Resource Manual, Washington, D.C.: National Association of State Directors of Special Education, 1977.

Guide for Trainers: A Resource for Workshops on Developing Individual Education Programs, Washington, D.C.: National Association of State Directors of Special Education, 1977.

Guidelines for the Planning and Placement Team (PPT) and Its Role in Developing the Individualized Education Program (IEP), Hartford: Connecticut State Department of Education, June 1977.

Hayes, J., & Higgins, S. Issues regarding the IEP: Teachers on the front line, *Exceptional Children*, January 1978, pp. 267-273.

Hedbring, C., & Holmes, C. Getting it together with PL 94-142: The IEP in the classroom, *Education and Training of the Mentally Retarded*, October 1977, pp. 212-224.

"The IEP," *Education of the Visually Handicapped*, Fall 1977, pp. 95-96.

The IEP and personnel preparation (from the 1977 annual report of the National Advisory Committee on the Handicapped), *American Education*, October 1977, pp. 6-8.

Implementation Procedure for IEP/IDP Folders, Greensboro: Creative Activities, Inc., 1977.

Individual Education Programs for Idaho's Exceptional Children, Boise: Idaho Department of Education, May 1977.

Ling, D. *et al.* Individualized educational programming for hearing-impaired children, *The Volta Review*, May 1977, pp. 204-212.

Lovitt, T. The who, where and what of IEP's, *Early Years*, September 1977, *8*(1), 49-52.

Lovitt, T. Writing the IEP, *Early Years*, December 1977, *8*(4), 44-45, 50.

McCormack, J. Developing individualized educational plans for severely handicapped learners: The promises and the problems, Hightstown, N.J., Education of Severely and Profoundly Handicapped Children and Youth (conference sponsored by the Northeast Regional Resource Center), 1977.

National Advisory Committee on the Handicapped. Implementing the IEP concept, *American Education*, August/September 1977, pp. 6-8.

Parents and public law 94-142, *Newsounds*, June 1977, *2*(5), 1-7.

Policies for the development of written individual education programs, *Volta Review*, September 1977, *79*(5), 347-348.

Prospects of IEP's for gifted increasing, *Insights*, April 1977, *4*, 6.

Weintraub, F.J. Understanding the individualized education program (IEP), *Amicus*, April 1977, pp. 26-31.

Yoshide, R.K. et al. Evaluation of Education for the Handicapped, *Phi Delta Kappan*, September 1977, pp. 59-60.

You have new rights—Use them! *Closer Look*, Fall 1977, pp. 1-8.

Chapter 8

How to Buy Educational Materials for the Mainstream Class

8

The materials that a teacher uses as educational vehicles significantly affect his student's learning progress. All effective teachers know what to look for when selecting educational materials. With most effective teachers, however, this skill has been developed by chance, rather than by design. Before a teacher can be said to "know" a material or a program, he should be able to answer nearly any question posed, and to know which questions are irrelevant to the material at hand. How many teachers could pass such a test? Material selection is rarely addressed in a teacher's formal training; nor is it a focus of the literature. A teacher is, thus, forced to analyze materials according to whatever insights his experience and training have afforded him.

The "Guide for Material Selection" in Exhibit 8-1 is intended as a step toward improving the state of consumer and professional selection of material.

READABILITY ANALYSIS

"Readability" is the relationship of the reading material to the abilities of the learner. (See also Chapter 4 for additional discussion.)

A measure which has received wide acceptability on the secondary level is the "FOG Index," developed by Weisman (1975). See Exhibit 8-2.

Exhibit 8-1 Guide for Material Selection

Scope
   The teacher should look at the comprehensiveness of the program.

Skill Sequencing
   "Sequence" is the order of the subject matter to be taught. In this area, it is important to consider whether the materials are "sequentially dependent" or "spiraled." "Sequentially dependent" means that the student must master each level before moving to the next level. The teacher should be aware that this format leaves him limited flexibility. A "spiraled" approach is such that a topic may be left for a time and returned to later.

Curriculum Pacing
   This aspect of the material directly affects the teacher's ability to individualize instruction using that material. The teacher of the LD adolescent should look for suggestions for adapting the material to the LD student, who often requires additional or different experiences.

Structure
   In general, the more highly structured the lessons, the less dependent is student success upon his teacher's experience and training. This general rule suggests that a highly structured program lends itself to use by teacher aides or volunteers working under teacher supervision.

Consumer Skill Level Required
   Is the training of the user an integral part of each unit? Many products make both explicit and implicit assumptions regarding the skill level of potential users. For example, training in learning disabilities is a prerequisite for successful use of material designed to remediate poor visual sequential memory. Pay close attention to the terminology used by the publisher. Material that's full of jargon or esoteric terminology, for example, would generally be appropriate for use only by quite experienced teachers.

Exhibit 8-1 continued

Material Format
The material's format is another prime consideration for the mainstream teacher. The size of type and the arrangements of page type are important factors for a student whose disability is a visual one. Is the material in kit, book, or worksheet format? A student may feel overwhelmed when presented an entire book, yet experience success with completion of a single workbook page.

Independent Student Use
For the teacher of the mainstreamed LD adolescent, a common problem is to balance the need to individualize instruction for the LD student and the need to provide educational experiences for the remainder of the class. Materials which allow each student to work at his own pace—to either acquire or reinforce a concept or skill—are of particular importance. The teacher should also focus attention on the publisher's suggestions for evaluating and monitoring the student's progress.

Diagnostic Components
Materials which provide ways to pinpoint a student's skills and to identify areas in which the teacher should direct activities are essential with the mainstreamed LD student whose educational profile is characterized by peaks and valleys. The teacher should look for the inclusion of pre-tests and post-tests. The material should provide for continuous assessment during the instructional sequence.

Readability and Interest Level
A teacher at the secondary level should determine the readability of each textbook he is contemplating for use with a class of students. Teachers often find that texts targeted for a group of students on a specific grade level actually have a readability more suitable for students one or more grades higher. Determining readability is relatively simple, and the time and effort required can save both the teacher and students from great frustration in the long run.

Source: A Basic Q-Sheet for Analyzing and Comparing Curriculum Materials and Proposals. *Journal of Learning Disabilities.* Ed. Virginia Brown. August/September (1975), *8:* 408-416.

Exhibit 8-2 The Three-Step FOG Index

1. Take several samples of 100 words each, spaced evenly through-out the material. Count the number of sentences in each sample. (Stop the sentences count with the sentence ending nearest the 100-word limit.) Divide the total number of words in the sample (100) by the number of sentences. This gives you the average sentence length. Record this figure.

2. Using the same samples, count the number of words that have three or more syllables. Do not count words that are:
   a. Capitalized
   b. Combinations of short, easy words (e.g., bookkeeper)
   c. Verb forms made into three syllables by adding—ed, es.
      Record this number directly under the figure obtained in the first step.

3. The FOG Index is determined by totalling the two factors just recorded (average sentence length and number of three-syllable words in the sample and multiplying the total by 0.4 (four tenths). This gives you the approximate grade level of the written material. This estimate tends to run somewhat high with more difficult materials.

Source: Reprinted from *A Handbook for Developing Vocational Programs and Services for Disadvantaged Students* by L. Weisman, by permission of the Springfield Office of Education, 1978.

Informal Reading Inventories

Another strategy to determine the LD adolescent's reading ability is to use an Informal Reading Inventory (IRI).

Using an IRI, the teacher can observe his student's oral and silent reading at several difficulty levels.

An IRI consists of (1) samples from the materials used in the subject area and (2) comprehension questions. The student's reading ability is determined at four levels.

1. *Independent level*—the level at which the student can read independently (without instruction) with at least 99 percent accuracy in word recognition and 90 percent in comprehension
2. *Instructional level*—the level at which the student can read with teacher assistance
3. *Frustration level*—the level at which the student cannot read with adequate comprehension
4. *Hearing capacity level*—the level at which the student can comprehend 75 percent of the material read to him

Advantages of an Informal Inventory

The reading levels determined through the IRI approach are more reliable than those determined through the use of standardized methods, since IRI uses the actual teaching materials.

The structure of an IRI enables the teacher to vary the difficulty levels of materials and skills.

Since the materials used are those projected for use with the student, there is no additional expense required.

How to Prepare an IRI

There are several variations in the preparation of an IRI (see Otto and Smith, 1970 for example). The basic format however is similar in all the approaches. This is presented below:

1. The first step for the teacher in preparing an IRI is to select passages from ascending difficulty. The length varies as a function of the grade-level of the books—the more advanced the level the longer the passage. For the adolescent choose passages of approximately 150 words in length.

2. The teacher should then develop questions which are to measure the student's comprehension on the material. It is important that a determination be made of the student's understanding of vocabulary in addition.
3. The teacher should begin the student at a level where he can deal comfortably with both vocabulary and comprehension.
4. Reading samples should be taken of the student's oral and silent reading performance. In oral reading the focus is on the student's word attack skills. With silent reading, it is on comprehension.

Examples of oral reading errors the teacher should note include:

a. substitutions - words read "in place" of the actual word.
b. insertions - words interjected into the passage.
c. omissions - words left out of the passage.
d. repetitions - repetition of words or phrases.

The student's reading levels are then determined:

- *The Independent Level* - where the student can read with 99 percent accuracy in word attack and with 90 percent comprehension.

- *Instructional Level* - where the student can read with 95 percent accuracy in word attack and 70 percent comprehension ability. This is the level at which the teacher should begin instruction.

- *Frustration Level* - where the student reads with less than 90 percent word attack ability and less than 50 percent comprehension.

- *Hearing Capacity Level* - (also called Reading Potential Level) the highest level, where the student can comprehend 70 percent of the material read to him. This level represents the student's "potential" reading level if there were no mechanical problems involved with the reading.

- *Comparative Cost* - every teacher quickly learns, in view of limited budgets, the need to select materials carefully. This is particularly true with respect to consumable products. The teacher should compare the cost-effectiveness of various materials before selecting any one of them. Instructional personnel should also consider the feasibility of teacher-made alternatives.

- *Material Durability* - consider the packaging of the material, its construction, its life expectancy, and its viability for the intended student population.

- *Target Population* - the Student Guideline to the Selection of Instructional Materials is derived from the National Center on Educational Media and Material for the Handicapped.

Student Screen

A. Demographic Data
   1. Age _____
   2. Sex _____
   3. Instructional/developmental level _____
   4. Language development or preference _____
   5. Interest level _____

B. Limiting Conditions
   Preferred modalities _____
   Affective/behavioral considerations _____
   Strength areas _____
   Deficit areas _____

It is important to consider the characteristics of the students for whose use the materials are targeted. The following exhibit (8-3) is offered to assist teachers in materials selection.

Exhibit 8-3 Learner Characteristics As Considerations in Selection of Materials

1. What modes of input may the teacher employ?
   ____ auditory   ____ tactile
   ____ visual   ____ kinesthetic

2. What are the student's preferred modes of input?
   ____ auditory   ____ kinesthetic
   ____ visual   ____ multisensory
   ____ tactile

3. What are the student's possible modes of response?
   ____ verbal   ____ written   ____ gesture

4. What is the student's instructional level?_____

5. What is the student's reading level?_____

6. What is the student's interest level?_____

7. What are the student's interest areas? _____

8. What are the student's interest/motivation requirements?
   ____ use of a game-type format ____ use of novelty
   ____ use of humor   ____ use of an interactional
   ____ use of variety of stimuli   system of feedback
   ____ use of suspense
   ____ use of characters   ____ use of puppets
   ____ use of cartoon format

9. What are the student's entry skills? _____

10. What are the student's reinforcement requirements? _____

Source: Adapted from the National Center on Educational Media and Materials for the Handicapped Publication. Washington, D.C.: Department of Health and Human Services, 1972, pp. 1-2.

Organizing Curriculum Materials

Once materials are selected, the teacher's task is to organize them for their most effective use. The organization's format should enable both the student and the teacher to locate easily what they need, when they need it.

To achieve this objective, the following factors must be considered:

1. *Usage of materials*—The sensory channel through which the material is introduced, as well as the mode (visual, verbal, or motor) required of the student in responding, must be incorporated into the student's lesson plan.
2. Emphasize the *individuality of the student* in the learning process. The student who is attempting to cope with "normal" adolescent crises in addition to his learning disability must be considered in his totality, as well as in his specificity.
3. The *teacher is the catalyst* that determines the success of the material with a given student. It is the teacher who is cognizant of the learner, the learning situation, and the subject matter to be taught. It is essential that the teacher be aware of the powerful effect he exerts on a student's learning.
4. After the teacher has considered his role, the student's individuality, the manner of presentation, and the mode of response, there are three basic factors to address:
   A. *Appropriateness:* This factor relates to the student's level of cognitive ability. The teacher should ask questions such as: "Does this material require the student to evaluate the content?" and "What is the student's level of comprehension?" The material's difficulty should reflect the student's ability.
   B. *Social acceptability:* The student's chronological age, as well as his ability level, should be considered in determining the appropriateness of material.
   C. *Validity:* The relevance and accuracy of the material's content are of particular importance with the LD student. Material that is inherently meaningful is more easily retained by exceptional students.

Teacher Responsibility

Teacher training programs for the most part prepare teachers to instruct students of a specific age or grade in a specific subject. Regular education training seldom addresses the issue of coping with the needs of the mainstreamed LD adolescent. The individuality of the LD student is seen as an exception to generally accepted "universal similarities" (such as Piaget's concepts of cognitive development and Bloom's taxonomy of cognitive levels of functioning).

Every teacher should develop skills that help him use available information in the most efficient manner. Two basic activities must be the focus of a teacher's planning:

1. accurate diagnosis of the differences within and between individual learners within the classroom.
2. classification and organization of curriculum materials to allow individualized instruction within a regular classroom.

- Special considerations must be given to the stage of adolescence in planning a remedial program. It is essential that for the older student who has not yet achieved at least a sixth grade level of competence in math and language arts there be direct instruction in the basic skills in these areas.

- The remedial program must be both comprehensive, yet integrated in approach.

- For the LD adolescent there must be a curriculum balance between academics and career education so that the program both remediates the student's specific academic deficits and prepares him for post-high school career pursuits.

Goodman and Mann (1976) had suggested an outline for an alternative program (as opposed to the process-oriented approach) to correct the LD adolescent's academic deficiencies.

MEDIA

Professional growth is a lifetime task, and the ability to alter instruction systematically to produce a predictable and controlled result is the goal of effective teaching.

One way that a teacher can broaden his instructional options is to incorporate media into his planning for the LD student.

Instructional messages that will help the teacher store and retrieve material when appropriate may be categorized by subject, grade level, lesson, modality, equipment, and average length of lesson. For example:

> Subject: History
> Grade Level: 9-10
> Lesson: American Indians
> Modality: Visual and auditory
> Equipment: Filmstrip with cassette
> recording
> Average length: 35 minutes

Listing of Organizations that Offer Media Materials

On the following pages, you will find an annotated list of organizations that produce media materials in various subjects.

Social Studies

Davco Publishers
8154 Ridgeway Avenue
Skokie, IL 60076

Filmstrips and cassettes
on the various presidents
of the U.S.

Pendulum Press
Academic Building
Saw Mill Road
West Haven, CT 06516

History Filmstrip Library
with cassettes covering the
New World from 1500-1750 to
America today 1945-76.

Opportunities for Learning
8950 Lurline Avenue
Dept. 9AB
Chatsworth, CA 91311

Multimedia programs with
cassettes or records on
society, culture, and government.
Also includes transparencies (kits)
on various areas of history.

Xerox Education Publications
1250 Fairwood Avenue
P.O. Box 2639
Columbus, OH 43216

Multimedia kits on freedom
issues, trial, search and
seizure, free press, the right
to carry arms, Declaration of
Independence.

Educational Supplements
401 Westport Avenue
Norwalk, CT 06851

Numerous materials on explorers,
adventures in history. Current
issues in society.

Troll Associates
401 Westport Avenue
Norwalk, CT 06851

Numerous materials on American
history, biography, ancient
civilizations, colonial explorers,
geography, Indians, production
and resources, world history.

National Book Company
1019 S.W. Tenth Avenue
Portland, OR 97205

Materials on economics, Indians,
labor movements, nations, and
various areas of government.

Educational Design, Inc.
47 West 13th Street
New York, NY 10011

Cross-cultural global and ethnic
study units. Physical geography
and environmental studies.

Encyclopedia Britannica
    Educational Corporation
425 North Michigan Avenue
Chicago, IL 60611

Many multimedia kits on geography,
history, government, and
current affairs.

Classroom World Productions
14 Glenwood Avenue
Raleigh, NC 27602

Cassette tape programs on the
world around us, American
women, democracy, government,
early history, voting, impeachment.

Guidance Associates
41 Washington Avenue
Pleasantville, NY 10570

Kits and filmstrips on various
areas of history and current
affairs.

MultiMedia Productions, Inc.
P.O. Box 5097
Stanford, CA 94305

Audiovisual programs on
various subjects.

Current Affairs
24 Danbury Road
Wilton, CT 06897

Filmstrips with records on
various subjects.

Coronet Instructional Media
65 East South Water Street
Chicago, Il 60601

Various materials on
European history.

Educational Dimensions, Inc.
P.O. Box 126
Stamford, CT 06904

Various materials in many
areas.

Educational Audio Visual, Inc.
Pleasantville, NY 10570

Cassettes and filmstrips
on various subjects.

Eye Gate House, Inc.
146-01 Archer Avenue
Jamaica, NY 11435

Various materials.

Scott Education Division 5 Lower Westfield Road Holyoke, MA 01040	Filmstrips and records covering history and current events.
Caedmon 1995 Broadway New York, NY 10023	Cassettes and records on assorted subjects.
Paramount Pictures Corp. 5451 Marathon Street Hollywood, CA 90038	Sound filmstrips.
Microfilm Corp. of America Dept. G E 21 Harristown Road Glen Rock, NJ 07452	Classroom programs on microfiche.
National Geographic Education Services 17th and M Streets, N.W. Washington, DC 20036	Multimedia kits, filmstrips, and records on various topics.
Scholastic Audio Visual 906 Sylvan Avenue Englewood Cliffs, NJ 07632	American Adventure filmstrip series for secondary-level students.

Science

Reader's Digest Services Educational Division Pleasantville, NY 10570	Filmstrip/cassette units
Opportunities for Learning 8950 Lurline Avenue Dept. 9AB Chatsworth, CA 91311	Various materials on energy, the human body, earth science, the solar system, biology, astronomy, and oceanography. Also mini-labs on crystal radio kits, electric motor kits, alarms, and flashlights.
Xerox Education Publications 1250 Fairwood Avenue P.O. Box 2639 Columbus, OH 43216	Multimedia kits on various areas of biology, earth science, ecology, physical science, and technology.

Troll Associates 401 Westport Avenue Norwalk, CT 06851	Tremendous amount of material related to many areas of science.
Educational Record Sales 157 Chambers Street New York, NY 10017	Filmstrips, cassettes, and trans-parencies in various areas.
National Book Company 1019 S.W. Tenth Avenue Portland, OR 97205	Various materials on atmosphere, energy, nuclear science, ocean-ography, physics, plants, and weather.
Educational Design, Inc. 47 West 13th Street New York, NY 10011	Basic electricity slide/sound shows, rocket and space travel materials, and science mini-labs for constructing things.
Audio Visual Narrative Arts, Inc. Box 9 Pleasantville, NY 10570	Material on health, drugs, and contraception.
Encyclopedia Britannica 425 North Michigan Avenue Chicago, IL 60611	Materials on biology, environment, geology, meteorology, oceanography, astronomy, physical science, and chemistry.
Classroom World Productions 14 Glenwood Avenue Raleigh, NC 27602	Materials on earth resources, nature, and the space program.
Guidance Associates 41 Washington Avenue Pleasantville, NY 10570	Media kits and filmstrips in various areas of science.
MultiMedia Productions, Inc. P.O. Box 5097 Stanford, CA 94305	Audiovisual programs in various areas.
Coronet Instructional Media 65 East South Water Street Chicago, IL 60601	Various materials.

Educational Audio Visual, Inc.
Pleasantville, NY 10570

Cassettes and filmstrips in
various areas.

Scott Education Division
5 Lower Westfield Road
Holyoke, MA 01040

Filmstrips and records.

Educational Dimensions, Inc.
P.O. Box 126
Stamford, CT 06904

Assorted filmstrips, slide sets,
and videotapes.

Paramount Pictures Corp.
5451 Marathon Street
Hollywood, CA 90038

Sound filmstrips.

National Geographic Education
    Services
17th and M Streets, N.W.
Washington, DC 20036

Assorted media kits,
filmstrips, and records.

Clearview, Inc.
6666 N. Oliphant
Chicago, IL 60631

Multimedia kits and duplicating
masters on various topics.

General Lists

Audiovisual Instruction. Periodic listing of sources of evaluation. Department of Audiovisual Instruction, Association of Educational Communications and Technology, National Education Association, 1201 16th Street, N.W., Washington, DC 20036. Monthly (September-May), $12.00 per year.

Guides to Newer Educational Media: Films, Filmstrips, Kinescopes, Phono-Disc, Phono-Tapes, Programmed Instruction Materials, Slides, Transparencies and Videotapes, by Margaret Rufsvold and Carolyn Guss. Handbook describing available catalogs, lists, services, professional organizations, journals, and periodicals that regularly provide information on new educational media. Third edition, 1971.

Instructional Materials for Teaching Audiovisual Courses. Center for Instructional Communications (Film Rental Library), Syracuse University, Syracuse, NY 13210. 1968. $2.00.

Instructional Materials for Teaching the Use of the Library: A Selected Annotated Bibliography of Films, Filmstrips, Books and Pamphlets, Tests and Other Aids. Compiled by Shirley L. Hopkinson, Claremont House, San Jose, CA 95114. 1966. $1.00.

Sources of Audiovisual Materials, by Milbrey L. Jones. U.S. Government Printing Office, Washington, DC 20036. Order No.: FS 235:35090. 1967. 15 cents.

A Working Bibliography of Commercially Available Audiovisual Materials for the Teaching of Library Science, compiled by Irving Lieberman. Occasional Papers #94, University of Illinois, Graduate School of Library Science, Urbana, IL 61801. 1968. $1.00.

Reviews of new audiovisual materials also appear in *Booklist, Library Journal, School Library Journal,* and other education and library periodicals.

Lists of Films and Filmstrips

Educator's Guide to Free Films. Annual compilation of films available from industry and nonprofit organizations without charge. Educators Progress Service, Inc., Randolph, WI 53956. Annual. $10.75.

EFLA Evaluations. 1948 to date. Monthly listings on 3 × 5 cards. Educational Film Library Association, Inc., 250 West 57th Street, New York, NY 10019. Membership is $15 per year, plus service charge based on size of film library. (See below compilation in book form entitled *Film Evaluation Guide,* 1946-1965.)

8 Millimeter Film Directory, edited by G. Ann Kone for Educational Film Library Association. Distributed by Comprehensive Service Corporation, 250 West 64th Street, New York, NY 10023. 1969. $10.50.

Film Evaluation Guide. Encompasses the years of 1946-1964. Educational Film Library Association, Inc., 250 West 57th Street, New York, NY 10019. 1965. $30.00 Supplement for 1965-67, $10.00.

Film Library Quarterly. Includes articles and film reviews for libraries and film collections. Film Library Information Council, 101 West Putnam Avenue, Greenwich, CT 06830. Quarterly. $8.00 per year.

Film News. Monthly reviews and suggested uses for films and filmstrips. Published six times a year. Film News Co., 250 West 57th Street, New York, NY 10019. $6.00 per year.

Film Review Digest. Published four times a year. Educational Film Library Association, 250 West 57th Street, New York, NY 10019. Rates on request.

Index to 8 Millimeter Motion Cartridges. National Information Center for Educational Media. R.R. Bowker Co., 1180 Avenue of the Americas, New York, NY 10036. 1969. $16.00.

Index to 16 Millimeter Educational Films. National Information Center for Educational Media. R.R. Bowker Co., 1180 Avenue of the Americas, New York, NY 10036. 1969. $39.50.

Index to 35 Millimeter Educational Films. National Information Center for Educational Media. R.R. Bowker Co., 1180 Avenue of the Americas, New York, NY 10036. 1969. $34.00.

Landers Film Reviews. June 1956 to date. Monthly except July and August. (Annual volume available since 1965.) Landers Associates, P.O. Box 69760, Los Angeles, CA 90069. $35.00 per year, plus vinyl binder.

Silent Film Loop Source Directory. Lists silent 8-mm loop films by subject area, title, and educational level. Technicolor, Commercial and Educational Division, 1300 Frawley Drive, Costa Mesa, CA 92626. Free.

Sound Film Loop Source Directory. Lists sound 8-mm loops by subject, title, and educational level. Technicolor, Commercial and Educational Division, 1300 Frawley Drive, Costa Mesa, CA 92626. Free.

Lists of Overhead Transparencies

Source Directory, Prepared Transparencies. Lists transparencies by source, subject matter, and educational level. Graflex, Inc., 3750 Monroe Ave., Rochester, New York 14601. 1966. (Revised periodically.) $1.00.

Index to Overhead Transparencies. National Information Center for Educational Media. R.R. Bowker Co., 1180 Avenue of the Americas, New York, NY 10036. 1969. $22.50.

Lists of Tape and Disc Recordings

Educators' Guide to Free Tapes, Scripts and Transcriptions. Lists free audio materials by service, subject, and educational level. Educator's Progress Service, Inc., Randolph, WI 53956. Annual. $6.75.

National Audio Tape Catalog. Lists available tape recordings by title and subject. Department of Audiovisual Instruction, National Education Association, 1201 16th Street, N.W., Washington, DC 20036. 1967. $3.00.

Recordings for Children: A Selected List. Children and Young Adults Services Section, New York Library Association. Available from Mrs. Augusta Baker, New York Public Library, 20 West 53rd Street, New York, NY 10018. 1964. $1.00.

Lists of Programmed Instruction, Slides and Pictures

Learning from Pictures by Catharine M. Williams. A guide and source book on the use of pictures for all grade levels. Department of Audiovisual Instruction, National Education Association, 1201 16th Street, N.W., Washington, DC 20036. 1968. $4.50.

Programmed Learning: A Bibliography of Programs and Presentation Devices, edited by Carl H. Hendershot. Basic bibliography and 1967 and 1968 supplements, including vinyl binder and index. Order from Carl H. Hendershot, 4114 Ridgewood Drive, Bay City, MI 48707. $21.50.

Lists of Television Program Materials

Instructional Television Materials: A Guide to Films, Kinescopes Available for Televised Use. National Instructional Television Library Project, 10 Columbus Circle, New York, NY 10019. 1964. Free.

NCSCT Telecourse Catalog. The National Center for School and College Television, Box A, Bloomington, IN 47401. 1966. (Spring). Free.

REFERENCES

Goodman, L., & Mann, L. *Learning disabilities in the secondary school: Issues and practices.* New York: Grune and Stratton, 1976.

National Center on Educational Media and Materials for Handicapped. *Learner characteristics as considerations in selection of materials.* Washington, D.C.: Department of Health and Human Services, 1972, pp. 1-2.

Otto, W., & Smith, R.J. *Administering the school reading program.* Boston: Houghton Mifflin Co., 1970.

Weisman, L. *A handbook for developing vocational programs and services for disadvantaged students.* Springfield, Ill.: Springfield Office of Education, 1975.

SUGGESTED READINGS

A Basic Q-Sheet for Analyzing and Comparing Curriculum Materials and Proposals. Virginia Brown, Ed., *Journal of Learning Disabilities,* 1975, *8,* 408-416.

Armstrong, J.R. A model for materials development and evaluation. *Exceptional Child,* 1971, *38,* 327-334.

Baker, R.L., & Schutz, R.E. (Eds.): *Instructional product development.* New York: Van Nostrand Reinhold, 1971.

Cawley, J.F., & Vitello, S.J. A model for arithmetical programming for handicapped children. *Exceptional Child,* 1972, *39,* 101-110.

Ensminger, E.E. A proposed model for selecting, modifying or developing instructional materials for handicapped children. *Focus on Exceptional Children,* 1970, (9) *1,* 1-9.

Hammill, D.D., & Bartel, N.R. *Teaching children with learning and behavior problems.* Boston: Allyn and Bacon, 1975.

Hewett, F.M. *The emotionally disturbed child in the classroom.* Boston: Allyn and Bacon, 1968.

Johnson, D.J., & Myklebust, H. *Learning disabilities: Educational principles and practices.* New York: Grune and Stratton, 1967.

Scott, H.V. Comparing curriculum proposals. *Educational Leadership,* 1967, *25,* 242-248.

Smith, J.O., & Lovitt, T.C. Effects of instruction on an individual's verbal behavior. *Exceptional Child,* 1972, *38,* 685-693.

Thiagarajan, S., Semmel, D., & Semmel, N. *Instructional development for training teachers of exceptional children: A sourcebook.* Reston, Va.: Council for Exceptional Children, 1974.

Tyler, R.W. *Basic Principles of Curriculum and Instruction:* Chicago: Univ. Chicago Press, 1969.

Woodcock, R.W. Forty-five ways to teach reading. Paper presented to the Fifth International I.T.A. Conference, Hempstead, NY, Hofstra Univ., July 1968.

Definitions of a
Learning Disability

appendix A

Kirk, S.A. *Educating exceptional children.* Boston: Houghton Mifflin Co., 1962.

A learning disability refers to a retardation, disorder, or delayed development in one or more of the processes of speech, language, reading, spelling, writing, or arithmetic resulting from a possible cerebral dysfunction and/or emotional or behavioral disturbance and not from mental retardation, sensory deprivation, or cultural or instructional factors. (p. 261).

Myklebust, H.R. *Psychoneurological learning disorders in children.* In S.A. Kirk and W. Becker (Eds.), *Conference on children with minimal brain impairment.* Urbana, Ill.: University of Illinois, 1963.

. . .we use the term "psychoneurological learning disorders" to include deficits in learning, at any age, which are caused by deviations in the central nervous system and which are not due to mental deficiency, sensory impairment, or psychogenecity. The etiology might be disease and accidents, or it might be developmental. (p. 27)

Bateman, G. *An educator's view of a diagnostic approach to learning disorders.* Learning disorders, Volume I. Jerome Helmuth (Ed.) Seattle, Washington: Seattle Seguin School, 1965.

Children who have learning disorders are those who manifest an educationally significant discrepancy between their estimated intellectual potential and the actual level of performance related to basic disorders in the learning processes, which may or may not be accompanied by demonstrable central nervous system dysfunction, and which are not secondary to generalized disturbance or sensory loss. (p. 220)

Clements, S.D. *Minimal brain dysfunction in children,* (NINDB Monograph No. 3, U.S. Public Health Service Publication No. 1415). Washington, D.C.: U.S. Government Printing Office, 1966.

> The term "minimal brain dysfunction syndrome" refers in this paper to children of near average, average, or above average general intelligence with certain learning or behavioral disabilities ranging from mild to severe, which are associated with deviations of function of the central nervous system. These deviations may manifest themselves by various combinations of impairment in perception, conceptualization, language, memory, and control of attention, impulse, or motor function.
> Similar symptoms may or may not complicate the problems of children with cerebral palsy, epilepsy, mental retardation, blindness, or deafness.
> These aberrations may arise from genetic variations, biochemical irregularities, perinatal brain insults or other illness or injuries sustained during the years which are critical for the development and maturation of the central nervous system, or from unknown causes. (pp. 9-10)

Kass, C. Conference on Learning Disabilities, Lawrence, Kansas, November 1966.

> A child with learning disabilities is one with significant intradevelopmental discrepancies in central-motor, central-perceptual, or central-cognitive processes which lead to failure in behavioral reactions in language, reading, writing, spelling, arithmetic, and/or content subjects.

Kirk, S.A. *The diagnosis and remediation of psycholinguistic abilities.* Institute for Research on Exceptional Children, University of Illinois, 1966.

> A learning disability refers to a specific retardation or disorder in one or more of the processes of speech, language, perception, behavior, reading, spelling, or arithmetic. (pp. 1-2)

Learning Disabilities Division Formulational Meeting, National Council on Exceptional Children (C.E.C.), St. Louis, Mo., April, 1967.

> A child with learning disabilities is one with adequate mental abilities, sensory processes and emotional stability who has a limited number of specific deficits in perceptive, integrative, or expressive processes which severely impair learning efficiency. This includes children who

have central nervous system dysfunction which is expressed primarily in impaired learning efficiency.

National Advisory Committee on Handicapped Children, *Special education for handicapped children: toward fulfillment of the nation's commitment* . . . (1st annual report). Washington, D.C.: Department of Health, Education, and Welfare, 1968.

Children with special learning disabilities exhibit a disorder in one or more of the basic psychological processes involved in understanding or in using spoken or written languages. These may be manifested in disorders of listening, thinking, talking, reading, writing, spelling, or arithmetic. They include conditions which have been referred to as perceptual handicaps, brain injury, minimal brain dysfunction, dyslexia, developmental aphasia, etc. They do not include learning problems which are due primarily to visual, hearing, or motor handicaps, to mental retardation, emotional disturbance or to environmental disadvantage.

Learning-Disability Terminology

appendix B

Aphasia—impairment of the ability to use or understand oral language. Types include expressive, receptive, congenial, and acquired.

Apraxia—difficulty in motor output or in performing purposeful motor movements. Reflects an abnormality of the central nervous system.

Auditory blending—the ability to synthesize the phonemes of a word when it is pronounced with separations between phonemes.

Auditory perception—the ability to interpret or organize the sensory data received through the ear.

Basal reader approach—a method to teach reading in which instruction is given through the use of a series of basal readers. The sequence of skills, content, vocabulary, and activities are determined by the authors of the series.

Binocular difficulties—a visual impairment due to the inability of the two eyes to function together.

Body image—an awareness of one's own body and the relationship of the body parts to each other and to the outside environment.

Brain-injured child—a child who before, during, or after birth has received an injury to, or suffered an infection of, the brain. As a result, there are disturbances which prevent or impede the normal learning process.

Cerebral dominance—the control of activities by the brain, with one hemisphere usually considered consistently dominant over the other. In most individuals, the left side of the brain controls language function, and the left side is considered the dominant hemisphere. The right side is responsible for motor function.

Clinical teaching—an approach to teaching that attempts to "tailor make" learning experiences for the unique needs of a particular child.

Cloze procedure—a technique used in testing, teaching reading comprehension, and determining readability. It involves deletion of words from the text and leaving blank spaces, which the student fills by supplying the missing words.

Cognition—the act or process of knowing. The various thinking skills and processes are considered cognitive skills.

Concept—an abstract idea generalized from particular instances.

Cross-modality perception—the neurological process of converting information received through one input modality to another system within the brain. The process is also referred to as intersensory transfer, intermodal transfer, and transducing.

Developmental imbalance—a disparity in the developmental patterns of intellectual skills.

Developmental reading—the pattern and sequence of normal reading growth and development in a child in the process of learning to read.

Dyscalculia—inability to perform mathematical functions, usually associated with neurological dysfunction.

Dyslexia—a disorder of children who, despite conventional classroom experience, fail to attain the skills of reading.

Echolalia—the parrot-like repetition of words or phrases or sentences spoken by another person, without understanding the meaning of what is said.

Electroencephalograph—an instrument for graphically recording and measuring electrical energy generated by the cerebral cortex during brain functioning.

Endogenous—hereditary.

Etiology—the cause or origin of a condition.

Exogenous—resulting from factors other than heredity (such as environment or trauma).

Expressive language skills—speaking and writing skills required to produce language for communication with other individuals.

Figure-ground perception—the ability to attend to one aspect of the visual field while perceiving it in relation to the rest of the field.

Grapheme—a written language symbol that represents an oral language code.

Hyperkinesis—constant and excessive movement and motor activity.

Hypokinesis—the absence of a normal amount of bodily movement and motor activity; extreme lack of movement; listlessness.

Impulsivity—the behavioral characteristic of acting upon impulse without considering the consequences of the action.

Innate response system—the unlearned motor responses that the child has within him at birth.

Inner language—the process of internalizing and organizing experiences without the use of linguistic symbols.

Integrative learning—the type of learning in which all modality systems function simultaneously and as a unit.

Interneurosensory learning—learning that results from the interrelated function of two or more systems in combination.

Language arts—school curricular activities that utilize language; namely, listening, speaking, reading, writing, handwriting, and spelling.

Language-experience approach to reading—a method of teaching reading and other language skills, based on the experience of the child.

Laterality—the awareness of the two sides of one's body, and the ability to identify them as left and right.

Learning disabilities—one or more significant deficiencies in essential learning processes, requiring special educational techniques for its remediation. The LD child demonstrates a discrepancy between expected and actual achievement in one or more areas. The LD child is not primarily the result of sensory, motor, intellectual, or emotional handicap, or lack of opportunity to learn.

Linguistics—the scientific study of the nature and function of human language.

Maturational lag—a slowness in certain specialized aspects of neurological development.

Memory—the ability to store and retrieve upon demand previously experienced sensations and perceptions, even when the stimulus that originally evoked them is no longer present. Also called imagery or recall.

Minimal brain dysfunction—a mild or minimal neurological abnormality that causes learning difficulties in the child with near-average IQ.

Mixed laterality—tendency to perform some acts with a right-side preference, and others with a left; or, shifting from right to left for certain activities.

Modality—a pathway through which an individual receives information and, thereby, learns. The modality concept postulates that some individuals learn better through one modality than through another.

Morpheme—the smallest meaning-bearing unit in a language.

Morphology—the system of meaning-units in a language.

Ocular pursuit—eye movement that is the result of visually following a moving target.

Oracy—the communication skills of oral language: listening and speaking.

Perception—the process of organizing or interpreting the raw data obtained through the senses.

Perceptual disorder—a disturbance in the awareness of objects, relations, or qualities involving the interpretation of sensory stimulation.

Perceptually handicapped—a term applied to the person who has difficulty in learning because of a disturbance in his perception of sensory stimulation.

Perceptual-motor—a term describing the interaction of motor activity and the various channels of perception. The channels of perception include visual, auditory, tactile, and kinesthetic.

Perseveration—the tendency to continue an activity once it has been started and to be unable to modify or stop the activity even though it is acknowledged to have become inappropriate.

Phoneme—the smallest unit of sound in any particular language.

Phonetics—the study of all the speech sounds in language and how these sounds are produced.

Phonics—the application of portions of phonetics to the teaching of reading.

Phonology—the linguistic system of speech sounds in a particular language.

Programmed reading—a method of teaching reading that uses programmed self-instructional and self-corrective materials.

Psycholinguistics—the field of study that blends aspects of two disciplines— psychology and linguistics—to examine the total language process.

Readability—an indication of the difficulty of reading material in terms of the grade level at which it is expected to be read successfully.

Receptive language—language that is spoken or written by others and received by the individual: listening and reading.

Sensory-motor—a term referring to the combination of sensory input and motor output; i.e., what is happening to the sensory organs at the time of visual, auditory, tactile, or kinesthetic sensations.

Social perception—the ability to interpret stimuli in a social environment and to relate appropriately such interpretations to the social situation.

Soft neurological signs—neurological abnormalities that are mild or slight and difficult to detect.

Strauss Syndrome—a collection of behavioral characteristics describing the child who has difficulty in learning.

Strephosymbolia—perception of visual stimuli, especially words, in reversed or twisted order.

Tactile perception—the ability to interpret and give meaning to sensory stimuli that are experienced through the sense of touch.

Visual-motor coordination—the ability to coordinate vision with the movements of the body or parts of the body.

Visual perception—the identification, organization, and interpretation of sensory data received by the individual through the eye.

Appendix C
Annotated Materials Bibliography

appendix C

Teacher's Choice (1976)
Peter Dublin, Editor
Institute of Open Education
Cambridge, MA 02138
   This is an annotated bibliography of educational materials used in pre-kindergarten through grade twelve. The 168-page, soft-cover catalogue includes descriptions from teachers who have used the materials in their classrooms, as well as technical reviews. Drawings and photographs further illustrate these teacher-selected resources.

Workshop: Creating Instructional Materials for Handicapped Learners (Developed by Northwest Special Education Instructional Materials Center) (1975)
National Audiovisual Center (NAC)
National Archives and Record Service
Sales Order Desk
General Services Administration
Washington, DC 20409
   This training workshop for teachers of handicapped children is presented in two sessions. The first session requires seven to eight hours, and concerns adapting and improvising instructional materials. The second session, a two-hour follow-up, is used to evaluate the instructional materials the teachers have adapted or improvised and tested in their classrooms.
   Included in the workshop kit are a Coordinator's Guide, activity sheets, a single cassette tape, and two sound filmstrips. The Coordinator's Guide provides complete instructions for planning and presenting the workshop. The handouts are bound into the Guide and must be duplicated. The titles of the filmstrips are "Selecting Instructional Materials" and "Educating Young Handicapped Chil-

dren: Getting the Most Out of Materials.'' The cassette tape is an eight-minute lesson on creativity.

Included: Coordinator's guide   Equipment   Cassette tape player
           2 Filmstrips   needed: Filmstrip projector
           3 Cassette tapes

How to Make a Black and White Filmstrip (1976)
Walt Taranko
Special Education Resource Center
Bureau of Pupil Personnel
Connecticut State Department of Education
275 Windsor St.
Hartford, CT 06115

This sound filmstrip is part of a teacher-training program demonstrating filmstrip production. Students draw pictures and photograph their drawing, and the teacher develops the film as he explains the process.

Included: Cassette tape   Equipment   Cassette tape player
           Filmstrip   needed: Filmstrip projector
           Teacher's guide

Multiple Skills Series E 1 (1976)
Richard Boning
Lowell and Lynwood, Ltd.
965 Church Street
Baldwin, NY 11510

This controlled reader (50-page, soft-cover) is aimed at students reading at a fifth- or sixth-grade level. Fifty high-interest paragraphs are followed by five multiple-choice questions referring to the title, details, inferences, and vocabulary.

Scope Activity Kit–Radio (1975)
Scholastic Book & Magazine Service, Inc.
902 Sylvan Avenue
Englewood Cliffs, NJ 07632

This kit contains 30 student readers with short thematic units on the history of radio. The material is intended for students reading at a fourth- to sixth-grade level. Six ditto masters with written activities covering unit concepts are included. A teaching guide suggests additional small- and large-group reading activities.

Included: 30 Readers
          6 Ditto masters
          Teaching guide

Scope Activity Kit–Frauds & Hoaxes (1975)
Scholastic Book & Magazine Service, Inc.
902 Sylvan Avenue
Englewood Cliffs, NJ 07632
   This kit contains 30 student booklets with short thematic units on famous and fictional frauds and hoaxes. The stories are intended for secondary-level students reading at a fourth- to sixth-grade level. Written activities are included on six ditto masters. A teaching guide outlines suggestions for individual and small- and large-group activities.
Included: 25 Readers
            6 Ditto masters
            1 Teaching guide

Scope Activity Kit–Sports (1975)
Scholastic Book & Magazine Service, Inc.
902 Sylvan Avenue
Englewood Cliffs, NJ 07632
   This is a high-interest reading program with selections on sports for students of both sexes. The material is intended for students reading at a fourth- to sixth-grade level.
   There are 30 magazine readers, 6 ditto masters, and a teaching guide in this kit. Outlined on the ditto masters are individual student activities. The teaching guide suggests additional exercises.
Included: 30 Student readers
            6 Ditto masters
            Teaching guide

Organizational Skills and Following Directions (1974-1976)
Pirie and Pirie
Curriculum Associates, Inc.
94 Bridge Street
Newton, MA 02158
   The *Organizational Skills* workbook is designed for use in remedial language-arts classes. The lessons introduce and review the following organizational skills: smallest to largest; largest to smallest; developmental order; historical sequence; relationship of parts to the whole; time lines; main ideas; and sequences of ideas and events, sentences in paragraphs, and paragraphs in stories. Ten copies are available.
   The activities in the *Following Directions* workbook are aimed at helping students who need practice analyzing and organizing information for following directions. Some of the activities require students to write their own directions. It is

recommended that students work on these lessons in pairs, using their own workbooks. Ten copies are provided.

Included: 9 Organizational Skills workbooks
1 Teacher's guide
9 Following Directions workbooks
1 Teacher's guide

How to Make Overhead Transparencies (1976)
Walt Taranko
Special Education Resource Center
Bureau of Pupil Personnel
Connecticut State Department of Education
275 Windsor St.
Hartford, CT 06115

This is a teacher-narrated filmstrip and cassette program aimed at special-educators in elementary and secondary schools. Described are two different methods for making overhead transparencies, and suggestions for using student-made transparencies and the overhead projector in classroom instruction. This audiovisual program lasts approximately eight minutes.

Included: Cassette tape   Equipment   Cassette tape player
Filmstrip   needed: Filmstrip projector
Teacher's guide

Studying for a Driver's License (1973)
Donald Joyce
New Reader Press
Box 131
Syracuse, NY 13210

This is a 56-page, soft-cover, self-correcting study workbook for persons applying for a driver's license. It should be used in conjunction with the appropriate state motor vehicle manual. There are review questions, definitions, and sample tests representing each section of a state motor vehicle manual.

Driver Education Crossword Puzzles (1970)
Judith Musumeci
Ohio State University Press
Publications Sales Division
2070 Neil Avenue
Columbus, OH 43210

This 44-page, soft-cover book is written for the driver education student to acquaint him with driving terminology. The puzzles are arranged in increasing order of difficulty, with answers provided on the back of each page. A vocabulary list is provided at the end of the book.

Mott Basic Language Skills Program: Comprehension Series (1972)
Chapman et al.
Allied Education Council
Distribution Center
P.O. Box 78
Galien, MI 49113

The Comprehension Series is a collection of eight magazine workbooks with controlled reading levels (grade equivalents 2-7) and self-correcting questions. Each magazine contains high-interest short stories. Multiple-choice questions that tap understanding and retention of the written material are interspersed in the narratives.

Included: Book 301 Book 601
           Book 302 Book 602
           Book 303 Book 603
           Book 304 Book 604
           8 Cardboard sliders

How to Be a Word Detective (1975)
Ward Cramer, Suzanne Dorsey and August J. Mauser
Academic Therapy Publications
1539 Fourth Street
San Rafael, CA 94901

This is a guide to understanding the pronunciation and definition of new words. A separate Decoding Clue Card lists the most common letter combinations and their pronunciations.

Included: Soft-cover book (47 pp.)
           Decoding Clue Card

Complete Action Library (1974)
Miriam Lee
Scholastic Book Service
904 Sylvan Avenue
Englewood Cliffs, NJ 07632

The Action Reading Program was designed to stimulate the interest and reading enjoyment of junior and senior high school students reading below a fourth-grade level. In each kit there are duplicate copies of five different titles, with one teaching guide and ten spirit master worksheets per title. The breakdown in the readability ranges of the Library Kits is as follows: Libraries 1 and 1-A, 2.0-2.4; Libraries 2 and 2-A, 2.5-2.9; Libraries 3 and 3-A, 3.0-3.4; Libraries 4 and 4-A, 3.5-3.9.

Included: 8 Library kits which contain:
             20 Readers
             50 Spirit masters
             Teacher folder

Building Word Power (1975)
Sandra Brown
Modern Curriculum Press
13900 Prospect Road
Cleveland, OH 44136
   The program consists of one-page exercises in reading and sentence completion
to build understanding in the following areas: figurative language, trite words,
synonyms, antonyms, definitions, multiple meanings, and understanding words
through context. Answers are keyed on the last two pages.

Motocross Racing (1973)
Red Hallum
Educational Activities, Inc.
1937 Grad Avenue
Baldwin, NY 11510
   This reading package contains ten paperback readers, a filmstrip, a cassette
tape, and a teacher's guide. The filmstrip and cassette recording provide a word-
by-word narration of the story with live background noises and photographs taken
at a motocross racetrack. Vocabulary discussion questions and related activities
are outlined in the teacher's guide.
Included: 10 Readers   Equipment   Filmstrip projector
             1 Filmstrip   needed: Cassette tape player
             1 Cassette tape
             1 Teacher's guide

Holt Impact Series
Holt, Rinehart & Winston, Inc.
383 Madison Avenue
New York, NY 10017
   These eight paperback readers contain a combination of short stories, poems,
scripts, photographs, and drawings. Thematic units are constructed to stimulate
and help clarify the personal and social awareness of older students. Readability
levels vary.
Included: *Larger Than Life*
             Sight Lines

Conquests in Reading (1962)
William Kottmeyer, Kenneth Ware
Webster Division
McGraw-Hill Book Company
1221 Avenue of the Americas
New York, NY 10020

This soft-cover, 144-page workbook contains exercises for the student learning vowels, consonants, diphthongs, diagraphs, prefixes, suffixes, and other word building and decoding skills. At various levels of progress, there are sections containing short fables for practice in reading and using the skills acquired.

Dictionary (1973)
Hollis Wyks
Curriculum Laboratory
Vocational-Technical Education Department
Building 4103, Kilmer Campus
Rutgers University
New Brunswick, NJ 08903

This 21-page, soft-cover dictionary guide was written specifically for deaf students but could be used with students who require low-level reading material. The following topics are covered: alphabetizing, guide words, pronunciation, homographs, word beginnings and endings, grammatical abbreviations, and definitions. Understanding of these dictionary skills is tested at the end of the workbook.

Troubleshooter I (1975)
Patricia Benner and Virginia Law
Houghton Mifflin Company
One Beacon Street
Boston, MA 02107

There are eight self-directing student workbooks in this language-arts series. Each contains a pre-test, exercises, and two review tests. The instruction reviews consonants, vowels, spelling, word attack, word mastery, grammar, punctuation, and basic English used in daily situations.

Included: *Sound Out*
Sound Off
Spelling Action
Word Attack
Word Mastery
Sentence Strength
Punctuation Power
English Achievement

Troubleshooter II (1975)
Joel Weinberg and Patricia Benner
Houghton Mifflin Company
One Beacon Street
Boston, MA 02107

The Troubleshooter II program aims to develop reading and study skills. There are six self-directing workbooks in this series, which emphasizes word recognition, vocabulary, spelling, reading for comprehension, reading in specific subjects, and reading and study skills.

Included: *Word Recognition*
Vocabulary
Spelling
Reading and Comprehension
Reading in Specific Subjects
Reading and Study Skills

Reading Skill-Builder Program 1 (1973)
Reader's Digest Services, Inc.
Pleasantville, NY 10570

This paperback collection is intended for students reading first- to sixth-grade levels. There are four copies each of 14 different titles. Each magazine contains stories on topics of interest to high-school students. Self-correcting written exercises follow each narrative. The teacher's guide suggests methods for incorporating the independent skill-builder activities into an instructional program. Student placement and progress checks are also outlined.

Included: Master manual
3 Answer keys
56 Skill builder readers

Reading Skill-Builder Program 2 (1973)
Reader's Digest Services, Inc.
Pleasantville, NY 10570

Skill Builder 2 is a paperback book collection for high school students reading at seventh- to ninth-grade levels. The series includes four copies each of 12 different titles. Each magazine reader combines high-interest stories with written exercises. Answer keys allow self-correction. The master manual suggests specific placement and progress checks.

Included: 48 Skill builder readers
3 Answer keys
Master manual
Teacher's guide

Kit A–PAL Paperbacks (1976)
Xerox Education Publications
1250 Fairwood Avenue
P.O. Box 2639
Columbus, OH 43216

Kit A is a paperback book collection of high-interest reading material for students reading at 1.5-3.5 grade levels. There are three copies each of 18 different titles. Each book consists of short stories with themes that appeal to both sexes: adventure, science, magic, sports, cars, humor, and teen problems. The teacher's guide lists activities for each short story.

Included: 54 Paperback readers
            Teacher's guide

Reading Success Series (1969)
Carolyn Paine
Xerox Education Publications
1250 Fairwood Avenue
P.O. Box 2639
Columbus, OH 43216

The Reading Success Series is designed for students 10-16 years old. The series of magazines is numbered by skill steps beginning with Score 1. The Score numbers do not refer to reading grade levels, but to progressive steps in developing skills. Each magazine contains high-interest, low reading-level articles with skill-building exercises.

Included: 6 Magazines:
            Score 1 through Score 6

Basic Reading Skills (1968)
Marion Monroe, A. Steri Artley and Helen M. Robinson
Scott, Foresman and Company
Glenview, IL 60025

This package includes audiovisual material designed to develop basic word-study skills, comprehension skills, and study skills. The program is aimed at students who read at a fourth-grade level and require concentrated skill-building work and/or alternative instructional modes.

The kit consists of a student workbook, a teacher's edition of the workbook, 16 cassette tapes, and 49 overhead visuals.

Included: 16 Cassette tapes   Equipment needed:
            Skill lesson book   Cassette tape player
            Student workbook (word study) Overhead projector
            Student workbook: teacher's edition
            49 Overhead visuals

Target Reading (1973)
Major Armstead and Raymond Gerlik
Laidlaw Brothers Publishers
River Forest, IL 60305
　There are six workbooks in this high-interest, controlled readability series. The short stories are written at a mid-third- to low-seventh-grade level. Answer keys are included for each workbook.
Included:　Purple book & answer key
　　　　　　Red book & answer key
　　　　　　Orange book & answer key
　　　　　　Blue book & answer key
　　　　　　Green book & answer key
　　　　　　Gold book & answer key

Reading Attainment System 1 (1975)
Grolier Educational Corporation
845 Third Avenue
New York, NY 10022
　This system is the first of two programs designed for the older student who is reading below his grade level. It takes the student up to a reading level approximately equivalent to mid-fourth-grade. Reading selections are written on 120 cards color-coded by reading level. Each reading card has a corresponding skill card designed to measure and develop comprehension skills, vocabulary, and word-attack skills. Answer keys and record books allow the student to correct and record his own progress. The instructor's manual explains the use of each program component.
Included:　120 Graded reading selections
　　　　　　120 Skill cards
　　　　　　 30 Reader record books
　　　　　　120 Answer keys
　　　　　　　 1 Pronunciation guide wall chart
　　　　　　　 1 Instructor's manual

Reading Attainment System 2 (1975)
Created by Educational Design
Grolier Educational Corporation
845 Third Avenue
New York, NY 10022
　This reading program is aimed at high school students reading at high-fourth- to mid-sixth-grade levels. Reading selections are written on 120 heavy cards color-coded by reading level. Each reading card has a corresponding skill card designed to measure and develop comprehension skills, vocabulary, and word-attack skills.

Answer keys and record books allow the student to correct and record his own progress. The instructor's manual explains the use of each program component.

Included: 120 Reading cards
120 Skill cards
120 Answer keys
15 Record books
Instructor's manual
Pronunciation chart

Specific Skills Series (1976)
Richard Boning
Barnell Loft, Ltd.
958 Church Street
Baldwin, NY 11510

This is a seven-level reading program designed to develop the following reading skills at each level: understanding sounds, following directions, using the context, locating the answer, getting the facts, getting the main ideas, drawing conclusions, and detecting the sequence. Levels A-G correspond with reading levels 1-7. The teacher's manual suggests placement and progress checks and a possible recording system.

Included: Record chart
Spirit masters
56 Workbooks

Adventures All Around Us (1967)
Henry Bamman, M. Dawson, Robert Whitehead
Benefic Press
Chicago, IL 60600

This is a 255-page, hard-cover book to be used in conjunction with a basic reading program. The stories are short in length, but designed to extend the child's reading experience. Questions at the end of each story provide the student with practice in critical thinking and character evaluation. Each story emphasizes reading for content.

Included: 1 Student book
1 Teacher's edition

Reading Skill Cards (1969)
John Stone, William Kottmeyer, and Ann Ware
Webster Division
McGraw-Hill Book Company
1221 Avenue of the Americas
New York, NY 10020

This self-directing, self-contained program is intended to develop the reading skills of students reading at a second-through-eighth-grade level. The kit contains 224 graded reading selections with follow-up tests. Each selection is printed on one side of a card, with test questions on the reverse side. Analysis of the test answers indicates a student's capabilities and performance constraints.

Included: 224 Coded cards in cardboard box

Reading Incentive Program (1974)
Ed Radlauer and Ruth Radlauer
Bowmar Publishers
Colorado Blvd.
Los Angeles, CA 90039

This reading program has several components designed to stimulate the interests of reluctant readers. There are seven packages—each containing ten readers, a teacher's guide, a filmstrip, and a cassette tape. The titles are *Motorcycles, Slot Car Racing, Snowmobiles, Custom Cars, Minibikes, Drag Racing,* and *Drag Racing Funny Cars.* The filmstrips and cassette recordings follow the narrative in the readers, adding actual background sounds. The individual components may be used for individual, and small- and large-group activities. Suggestions to motivate the students and reinforce their learning are given in each teacher's manual.

Included: 7 packages, each containing: Equipment needed:
            10 Readers   Filmstrip projector
            1 Filmstrip   Cassette tape player
            1 Cassette
            1 Teacher's manual

Target Program (1974)
Harold Friedman and Corinne Bloomer
Educational Services
630 Fifth Avenue
New York, NY 10019

Each of the four units in the Target Program contains a filmstrip, a cassette tape, six paperback books, and a teacher's manual. The reading instruction, aimed at students 12 through 18 years of age who read at a third-grade level, uses baseball, basketball, football, and hockey as subject matter.

Included: 6 Student's Books   Equipment needed:
            Teacher's manual   Cassette tape player
            Cassette & filmstrip   Filmstrip projector

Points of View (1975)
Ann Elwood and John M. Raht
Globe Book Company, Inc.
175 Fifth Avenue
New York, NY 10010

This 229-page, soft-cover book consists of 25 very short stories. Each story is designed to stimulate the student in decision-making situations. Review questions, a vocabulary exercise, and open-ended thought questions are at the end of each story.

Language Skills Test (1972)
Margaret L. Deibler and Susan J. Riddle
Continental Press, Inc.
Elizabethtown, PA 17022

This program provides instruction and practice in four areas: basic language skills, language usage, vocabulary skills, and pre-dictionary skills. The program is designed for individual use. The instructor acts as a tutor, since the lessons are self-instructional.

Included: 24 Filmstrips

Equipment Needed:

24 Pre-test duplicating masters   Filmstrip projector
24 Post-test duplicating masters   Cassette tape player
2 Teacher's guides and answer keys

Useful Arithmetic: Volumes I and II (1973)
John D. Wool and Raymond J. Bohn
Frank E. Richards Publishing Co., Inc.
P.O. Box 66
Phoenix, NY 13135

The two volumes of this series are self-directing student workbooks designed for use in basic consumer-education classes. Exercises teach basic arithmetic skills necessary for using money in daily life. Teacher's editions of the two workbooks are included.

Included: *Useful Arithmetic: Volume I* (three copies)
Useful Arithmetic: Volume I
(Teacher's Edition)
Useful Arithmetic: Volume II (three copies)
Useful Arithmetic: Volume II
(Teacher's Edition)

Arithmetic That We Need (1969)
Thomas Mooney
Frank E. Richards Publishing Co., Inc.
P.O. Box 66
Phoenix, NY 13135
   The following problems are covered in this student workbook: measurement in inches, feet, and miles; liquid measures in cups, pints, and gallons; temperature in Fahrenheit degrees; deductions in pay checks; using money; Roman numerals; percentages; and clock time. A teacher's edition of the workbook is included.
Included: *Arithmetic That We Need* (three copies)
             Arithmetic That We Need
             (Teacher's Edition)

Using Money Series: Parts I-IV (1973)
John Wool
Frank E. Richards Publishing Co., Inc.
P.O. Box 66
Phoenix, NY 13135
   This series consists of four basic consumer-education workbooks. Book I introduces American coins and their values. Book II reviews the previous lesson, and provides for practice in counting change. Book III provides for practice in shopping economically. Book IV reviews the previous exercises and discusses how money is earned, budgeting, and various banking services.
Included: 3 copies each of the following
             Counting My Money
             Making My Money Count
             Buying Power
             Earning, Spending and Saving

The Learning Skills Series (1976)
William Hunter and Pauline L. LaFollete
Webster Division
McGraw-Hill Book Company
1221 Avenue of the Americas
New York, NY 10020
   These are four arithmetic workbooks designed for high-school students requiring remediation in addition, subtraction, multiplication, and division. Each workbook combines basic math problems with the normal experiences of high-school students. A few examples are: buying consumer goods, budgeting, figuring distances, and reading graphs.

Included: *Acquiring Arithmetic Skills*
            Building Arithmetic Skills
            Continuing Arithmetic Skills
            Directing Arithmetic Skills

Basic Elementary Mathematics: Set I (1971)
Ann Edson and Allan A. Schwartz
Educational Activities, Inc.
P.O. Box 392
Freeport, NY 11520
   This is a set of ten cassette tapes containing self-directing and self-correcting exercises in basic arithmetic operations. The series is suggested for use in remedial math classes as individual drill, small-group instruction, large-group instruction, or as an instrument to evaluate knowledge of basic math operations. The following arithmetic concepts are covered: addition, subtraction, multiplication, division, measurement, writing numerals, estimating, and problem solving.
Included: 10 Cassette tapes   Equipment   Cassette tape player
            10 Summary sheets   needed:

The Slow Learner in Mathematics
The National Council of Teachers of Mathematics, Inc.
1906 Association Drive
Reston, VA 22091
   This is a yearly publication that reviews learning activities, aids, and programs aimed at slow learners in mathematics classes. The 528-page, hard-cover book provides information on teaching slow learners, specific classroom activities, and administrative and management processes relevant to special-education math teachers. Appendix I describes additional activities and materials. Appendix II lists materials recommended by the Council.

Using Dollars and Sense (1973)
Charles H. Kahn and J. Bradley Hanna
Fearon Publishers, Inc.
Pitman Publishing Corporation
6 Davis Drive
Belmont, CA 94002
   The exercises in this 112-page, soft-cover workbook provide practice in addition, subtraction, multiplication, and division using dollars and cents.

Mott Basic Language Skills Program: Consumer Buying, Basic Numbers and Money (1975)
Allied Education Council
Distribution Center
P.O. Box 78
Galien, MI 49113
    The exercises in this 156-page, soft-cover, self-correcting workbook combine instruction in basic arithmetic operations and reading newspaper advertisements. Answers are given in the left margin.

Math Applications Kit (1971)
Science Research Associates, Inc.
259 East Erie Street
Chicago, IL 60611
    This kit presents a large number of programs and activities in science, sports and games, occupations, social studies, and everyday things that students can explore using elementary-school mathematics as the basic tool of investigation. The activity cards include questions and related activities.
Included: Activity cards
            1 Student handbook
            1 Teacher's handbook
            1 *The World Almanac, 1974*

Computates 7 (1973)
Science Research Associates, Inc.
259 East Erie Street
Chicago, IL 60611
    Level 7 of this math program contains 204 audio lessons organized in 11 modules that allow practice in whole-number operations and fractions. Modules 1-6 review skills usually learned in grades 1-6. Modules 7-11 extend the review and cover directed numbers, number sentences, functions, graphs, applications, and geometry.
    Each cassette lesson has an accompanying activity sheet that is used while listening to the tape. The teacher's guide lists the following information for individual lessons: objectives, length, summary, and materials needed.
    Computates 7 is packaged in a hard-cover, 3-ring binder containing 10 cassettes, a teacher's guide, and worksheets.
Included: 3 Ring binder with 10 cassettes
            Teacher's guide
            Worksheets are available

Figure It Out (1971)
Mary C. Wallace
Follett Publishing Company
1010 West Washington Boulevard
Chicago, IL 60607
    Figure It Out is a mathematics curriculum designed to guide the student from the simple addition of two numbers through concepts up to averages and word problems. The student's workbook is designed to discourage reading matter, and has been kept brief and not extremely detailed. The instructor's book contains more detailed explanations of various processes, so that the teacher may explain each concept in a way best suited to the needs and capabilities of various students.
Included: Book I workbook
            Book I instructor's book

Basic Mathematics: Set II
Ann Edson and Allan A. Schwartz
Educational Activities, Inc.
P.O. Box 392
Freeport, NY 11520
    This is a set of ten cassette tapes containing self-correcting lessons in basic math operations. Set II provides drill work in the following: writing decimals; rounding decimals; renaming fractions and decimals; renaming decimals and percentages; renaming percentages, fractions, and decimals; adding positive and negative numbers; subtracting positive and negative numbers; multiplying positive and negative numbers; and dividing positive and negative numbers.
Included: 10 Cassette tapes   Equipment   Cassette tape player
            10 Summary sheets   needed:

Pacemaker Arithmetic Program (1974)
Fearon Publishers, Inc.
Pitman Publishing Corporation
6 Davis Drive
Belmont, CA 94002
    The Pacemaker Arithmetic Program is designed to give the special-need pupil a foundation of basic skills. The lessons in each level of the program follow the same pattern of presenting materials in a series of organized, sequential steps. Level B is designed to teach numbers through ten, including zero. Level C is structured to review the number concepts taught in Level B, plus counting through 99, and to teach addition and subtraction facts from zero to ten. Level D is a review of Level C, and teaches money, time, the calendar, and addition and subtraction of two- and three-digit numbers.

Included: Level B teacher's manual
             184 Student worksheets on duplicator masters
             Level C teacher's manual
             136 Student worksheets on duplicator masters
             Level D teacher's manual
             133 Student worksheets on duplicator masters

Spellbound (1975)
Elsie T. Rak
Educators Publishing Service, Inc.
75 Moulton Street
Cambridge, MA 02138

This is a preparatory reading program intended for use with junior- and senior-high-school students identified as having specific language disability. Student workbook activities emphasize phonetic spellings and concrete explanations. The teacher's guide lists spelling dictations found effective by teachers of retarded and/or nonreading students.

Included: *Spellbound–Phonetic Reading and Spelling*
             Spellbound–Teacher's Manual

Power Over Words 1
Power Over Words 2 (1968)
Hetty P. Archer and Clista M.E. Dow
Educators Publishing Service, Inc.
75 Moulton Street
Cambridge, MA 02138

These are two teacher's manuals for individualized spelling programs beyond the third-grade level. Syllables, word endings and word beginnings, plurals, double consonants, vowels, and commonly misspelled words are the unit topics. The authors recommend selecting appropriate unit activities as the needs arise.

Systematic Spelling (1969)
Myron R. Williams
Edited & revised by Carl Caspar
Educators Publishing Service, Inc.
75 Moulton Street
Cambridge, MA 02138

This 32-page, soft-cover pamphlet for English teachers outlines 18 exercises to develop accurate spelling; dictionary abbreviations, frequently misspelled words, and common spelling rules are among the topics covered.

Remedial Training for Children with Specific Disability in Reading, Spelling, and Penmanship (1975)
Anna Gillingham and Bessie W. Stillman
Educators Publishing Service, Inc.
75 Moulton Street
Cambridge, MA 02138
　　This 344-page, hard-cover manual's approach to teaching reading and spelling is based on Gillingham's theory of language development. Single letters, letter combinations, and words are taught phonetically. Drill cards that accompany the text show single letters and letter combinations. The authors recommend modifying the lessons for students in junior and senior high school.
Included:　Phonetics drill cards
　　　　　　A key to the Gillingham manual

The Many Faces of Youth (1971)
Developmental Learning Materials
7440 Natchez Avenue
Niles, IL 60648
　　Included in this package are 12 large black-and-white and color photographs of teenagers experiencing different emotions. A discussion guide summarizes each poster and suggests small-group activities.

Guidelines for Employment Orientation Programs for Special Needs Students (1975)
Curriculum Laboratory
Rutgers University
Building 4103, Kilmer Campus
New Brunswick, NJ 08908
　　This 105-page, soft-cover book provides a basic curriculum by which students can build social and personal competencies and a broad base of skills. These skills—learned through "hands on" experience—help insure successful entry into employment in many fields.
　　The curriculum places occupations in clusters, with detailed outlines containing objectives, related job areas, basic skills, suggested practical work assignments, suggested equipment and supplies, and references. Work clusters include: bench work, food service, building custodian, clerical work, transportation, distribution and sales, construction trades, health service, and horticulture.

Vocational Entry-Skills Student Worksheets (1976)
Winifred Washburn
Academic Therapy Publications
20 Commercial Boulevard
Novato, CA 94947

Exercises in this self-directing workbook provide practice in the skills needed to locate, apply for, and hold a job. Section A reviews basic reading and writing skills. Section B reviews job-oriented resources. Section C is a personal skills checklist. Section D covers related living skills. The final chapter, Section E, concentrates on basic skills needed for several jobs a high school graduate might seek.

Included: 9 Student workbooks

Be Informed Series (1976)
New Readers Press
Box 131
Syracuse, NY 13210
    This is a series of 20 thematic units covering various adult responsibilities. The 20 booklets in two looseleaf binders are written at a third- to fourth-grade reading level. The following titles are found in Binder I: Personal Credit, Buying a Car, Owning a Car, Buying a House, Finding a Job, Reading Your Newspaper, Taxes, and Banking. Unit titles in Binder II are Mental Retardation, Marriage, Measurements, Wise Buying, Using the Library, Money, Drugs, Nutrition, Population, and Pollution. A teacher's guide in each binder suggests introductory and follow-up activities.

Getting Ready for Pay Day (1966)
Margaret W. Hudson and Ann A. Weaver
Frank E. Richards Publishing Co., Inc.
P.O. Box 66
Phoenix, NY 13135
    This self-directing student workbook (36 pages, soft-cover) is designed for use in a living-skills program. Practice exercises review banking services and the basic skills needed to open and maintain checking and savings accounts.

The Budget (1974)
James Lenox
Curriculum Laboratory
Rutgers University
Building 4103, Kilmer Campus
New Brunswick, NJ 08908
    Government, family, and personal budgets are the major topics in this 28-page, soft-cover workbook. Although designed for deaf junior high school students, other special-needs students may benefit from the instruction.

Introduction to Office Occupations (1974)
Carol Troutman
Curriculum Laboratory
Rutgers University
Building 4103, Kilmer Campus
New Brunswick, NJ 08908

The objectives of this 27-page, soft-cover manual are to introduce high school students to different kinds of jobs in the clerical field and to describe the skills and training necessary for each job category. The following office positions are described: billing clerk, cashier, duplicating machine operator, file clerk, mail clerk, messenger, payroll clerk, stock clerk, tabulating-machine operator, and typist. Student activities follow each section.

Getting Your Dollar's Worth (1974)
Wallace Shackell
Curriculum Laboratory
Rutgers University
Building 4103, Kilmer Campus
New Brunswick, NJ 08908

These narratives warn of advertising gimmicks and misleading ads, and discuss loans, contracts, warranties, guarantees, and consumer-protection services. Activities and discussion questions follow each presentation in this 68-page, soft-cover book.

Newspaper Reading
Gary Lawson
Lawson Book Company
9488 Sara Street
Elk Grove, CA 95624

"Hands on" exercises that teach the functions of a newspaper are described in this workbook for the low-reading student.
Materials Needed: Local newspaper

"Everyday Business" (1976)
Gary Lawson
Lawson Book Company
9488 Sara Street
Elk Grove, CA 95624

The "everyday business" examined in this 85-page, soft-cover workbook relates to banking, budgeting, buying, paying taxes, and shopping for insurance. The completed activities are intended to serve later as a reference. The reading level and vocabulary are controlled for the slow reader.

Handbook of Job Facts (1972)
Carole J. Lang
Science Research Associates, Inc.
259 East Erie Street
Chicago, IL 60611
   Handbook of Job Facts—a 134-page, hard-cover book—contains concise summaries of basic information on 300 major occupations. The information is arranged in chart form under headings that can be read at a glance. The following topics are covered: a brief description of typical duties, where jobs in that occupation are found, number of workers employed, education and training necessary, special qualifications necessary, ways to enter the field, opportunities for advancement, average earnings, and employment trends concerning supply and demand.

The Newspaper (1970)
Hollis W. Wyks and Charles M. Jochem
Curriculum Laboratory
Rutgers University
Building 4103, Kilmer Campus
New Brunswick, NJ 08908
   This 28-page, soft-cover book offers a simple explanation of the various sections of the newspaper, and explains how to use them. Within the book are a vocabulary list, problems to solve using the newspaper, a quiz, and a test. Projects for the entire class and for individual students are also suggested.

With World Heroes
Henry Bamman
Benefic Press
Westchester, IL 60153
   This text contains biographical sketches of 24 world-renowned figures. Vocabulary lists, thought questions, and suggested activities follow each description. The reading level ranges between fifth- and sixth-grade.
   Included: *With World Heroes*
               With World Heroes: Teacher's Edition

"Where It's At" (1973)
Gary Lawson
Lawson Book Company
9488 Sara Street
Elk Grove, CA 95624

This 81-page, soft-cover student workbook covers the fundamentals of map reading, and introduces a few geographic, cultural, and economic facts about different regions of the world. The vocabulary and reading level are controlled at an elementary level.

Color Me American (1967)
Gary Lawson
Lawson Book Company
9488 Sara Street
Elk Grove, CA 95624

This 80-page, soft-cover workbook attempts to explain the U.S. Constitution, the branches of the federal government, the Bill of Rights, and basic responsibilities of every American citizen. The vocabulary and reading level are controlled at an elementary level.

Action Kit for Action Map (1971)
Denoyer-Geppert Co.
5235 Ravensworth Avenue
Chicago, IL 60640

This program is designed to help the student put into perspective important geographic, historic, and economic relationships that contributed to the development of the United States. The format is activities-oriented and may be used with the entire class or by individual students.

Included: *Box I – Its Changing Weather*
Teacher resource cards
Student resource cards
1 Package weather pictures (8 picture weather wheels and 100 weather maps)
1 Package cardboard mountains (100 climate charts)
1 Package cloud models
1 Legend activity sheet (2 projection markers)
4 Plastic stands (1 paint brush)

Box I – Its People and Where They Live
Teacher resource cards
Student resource cards
100 Desk activity maps
8 Cardboard Indians
Duplicating masters

13 Large picture wheels
1 Cut-and-folding block

Box II – People, Ideas, and Things in Motion
Teacher resource cards
Student resource cards
Duplicating masters
9 Large picture wheels
100 Student action maps
6 Plastic stands
1 Legend activity sheet
9 Large picture wheels
12 Small picture wheels
1 Bag silver
1 Bag gold

Box II – What It's Made Of and How It's Used
Teacher resource cards
Student resource cards
Duplicating masters
1 Legend activity sheet
1 Package paper stand-ups
100 Student activity maps

News Lab II (1974)
Lorne R. MacKenzie
Science Research Associates, Inc.
259 East Erie Street
Chicago, IL 60611

News Lab II contains study-guide cards divided into eleven sections: World News, Local News, Sports, Advertisements, Editorials, Women's Pages, Business, Entertainment, Cartoons and Comic Strips, Special Features, and News Themes. Each card assigns two activities: one designed to develop skills and one designed with an open-ended concept.

The cards may be used for individual or group work. Students are encouraged to explore and evaluate various newspapers.

Included: Cassette tape (introduction)   Equipment needed:
World map spirit master   Cassette tape player
41 Student record envelopes
Skills chart
Student booklet

Getting It Together (1973)
Herman Goldberg and Bernard Greenberger
Science Research Associates, Inc.
259 East Erie Street
Chicago, IL 60611
    The selections in this reader explore problems encountered by people of all ages. Through the reading, discussion, and written exercises, students are intended to identify and clarify their values and better understand the value systems of others. Other reading skills are developed through the follow-up exercises in the student resource book.
Included: 2 Hard-cover readers
            2 Resource books
            1 Teacher's guide

Safe and Sound (1965)
Gary Lawson
Lawson Book Company
9488 Sara Street
Elk Grove, CA 95624
    This 83-page, soft-cover workbook is aimed at slow-learning students studying health and safety skills. The author discusses the consequences of sound family planning, prenatal care, baby care, accident prevention, and first aid.

Consequences: In Other People's Shoes (1975)
Peter McPhail
Argus Communications
7440 Natchez Avenue
Niles, IL 60648
    This is a package of 71 cards which depict conflict situations in the areas of personal safety, morality, cooperation and values. The illustrations are designed during values-clarification activities.

Appendix D
Mainstreaming References

appendix D

Coming Back . . . Or Never Leaving: Instructional Programming for Handicapped Students in the Mainstream. Anne Langstaff Pasanella and Cara B. Volkmer. 1977. Published by Charles E. Merrill Publishing Co., 1300 Alum Creek Drive, Box 508, Columbus, OH 43216. Text $9.95; Mediapak $135.00.

A textbook, teacher's guide, five color filmstrips, and cassettes comprise this kit, which is designed for pre-service and in-service teachers, kindergarten through grade 12. The text and media package illustrate how to integrate mildly handicapped pupils into the regular classroom, with emphasis on identification, referral, placement, assessment, instructional programming, and program evaluation. The audiovisual materials and training activities support the text by illustrating two case studies, actual team conferences, classroom events, and interviews with involved pupils.

National Instructional Materials Information Systems Bibliographies. Staff, National Center on Educational Media and Materials for the Handicapped. 1977-78. Published by NIMIS/NCEMMH, c/o Publications Sales Division, Ohio State University Press, 2070 Neil Avenue, Columbus, OH 43210. $59.00 per series. Order number 78:115.

These 26 reference documents contain abstracts of materials appropriate for handicapped children classified by specific content areas, exceptionalities, age or grade level, etc.

Titles of Individual Bibliographies
1. Early Childhood: Activity Books/Resource Guides (50 items); Order number 77:112; $3.00
2. Early Childhood Kits (80 items); 77:109; $3.00
3. Early Childhood: Psychomotor Skills (31 items); 77:114; $2.00
4. Learning Disabled: Number Concepts, Primary Grades (62 items); 77:110; $3.00

5. Learning Disabled: Perceptual Skills; 78:105; $3.00
6. Learning Disabled: Kits and Series, Perceptual Skills (60 items); 78:106; $3.00
7. Mildly Handicapped: Consumer Education, Secondary Level (82 items); 77:103; $3.00
8. Mildly Handicapped: Reading, Secondary Level (107 items); 77:105; $4.00
9. Mildly Handicapped: Career/Vocational Education, Secondary Level (155 items); 78:107; $4.00
10. Trainable Mentally Handicapped: Daily Living and Self-Care Skills (153 items); 77:108; $4.00
11. Trainable Mentally Handicapped: Protective Vocabulary (21 items); 77:106; $2.00
12. Severely Mentally Handicapped: Fine Motor, Eye-Hand Coordination (25 items); 78:109; $2.00
13. Severely/Profoundly Mentally Handicapped (36 items); 77:104; $2.00
14. Severely Mentally Handicapped: Gross Motor Skills (53 items); 78:110; $3.00
15. Severely Mentally Handicapped: Language (15 items); 78:111; $2.00
16. Severely Mentally Handicapped: Self-Care Skills (28 items); 78:112; $2.00
17. Severely Mentally Handicapped: Sensory Training and Perceptual Development (69 items); 78:113; $3.00
18. Physically Handicapped: Adaptive Devices (76 items); 77:111; $3.00
19. Hearing Impaired: Language Development and Reading Skills (167 items); 78:104; $4.00
20. Emotionally Disturbed: Affective/Social Development, Secondary Level (97 items); 78:103; $3.00
21. Deaf/Blind (88 items); 78:101; $3.00
22. Driver Education (62 items); 78:102; $3.00
23. Movement Exploration and Psychomotor Skills (23 items); 77:115; $2.00
24. Rehabilitation Aids (40 items); 77:113; $2.00
25. Speech and Language Development (75 items); 78:114; $3.00
26. Parents (Materials for Use with Children) (63 items); 78:108; $3.00

The Mainstreaming Series. Thomas N. Fairchild, Editor. 1977. Published by Learning Concepts, 2501 North Lamar, Austin, TX 78705. $89.25 (complete series), $5.95 per booklet. Order number 338.52.

This series consists of 15 paperback books ranging from 100 to 136 pages. Practical suggestions for enhancing the special child's personal and educational development are provided, with each book focusing on a single handicapping condition or a relevant topic regarding P.L. 94-142. The series uses cartoons to illustrate concepts.

Working with Parents: The Teacher's Best Friend. Leatha Mae Bennett and Ferris Henson. 1977. Published by Learning Concepts, 2501 North Lamar, Austin, TX 78705. $49.95 per workshop kit. Order number 360-09.

This workshop kit contains a filmstrip, cassette, leader's guide, and participant manual. Central objectives are to train participants to build their skills in communicating with parents and to improve techniques of working with parents to maximize their input into the educational process. The kit uses cartoons to illustrate concepts. It may be used in one to three hours.

Standard Criteria for the Selection and Evaluation of Instructional Materials. Staff, National Center on Education Media and Materials for the Handicapped. 1976. Published by NCEMMH, c/o Publication Sales Division, Ohio State University Press, 2070 Neil Avenue, Columbus, OH 43210. Price available on request.

This seven-page checklist describes criteria for selecting and evaluating instructional materials for individuals and groups of handicapped learners.

Guide to Finding Appropriate Instructional Materials: Existing Retrieval Systems. James McCormick, Cathy Doyle, and Jody Blieberg. 1977. Published by Massachusetts Center for Program Development and Evaluation, 10 Hall Avenue, Medford, MA 02155. Price available on request.

This 27-page booklet provides a descriptive analysis of 11 instructional materials information retrieval systems, including their advantages, disadvantages, and characteristics.

Approaches to Mainstreaming: Teaching the Special Child in the Regular Classroom, Unit 1. Joyce Cejka and Frances Needham. 1977. Published by Teaching Resources Corporation, 100 Boylston Street, Boston, MA 02116. $76.00.

Four filmstrips, four cassettes, and a guide comprise this kit designed to provide in-service training for regular-classroom teachers who may have little or no background and experience with special-needs students. Information and suggestions are presented simply and clearly, focusing on individual differences, characteristics of children with special needs, organizing the classroom, and handling behavioral problems.

Approaches to Mainstreaming: Teaching the Special Child in the Regular Classroom, Unit 2. Joyce Cejka and Frances Needham. 1977. Published by Teaching Resources Corporation, 100 Boylston Street, Boston, MA 02116. $76.00.

This kit of four sound filmstrips and a 42-page guide is designed to provide in-service training for regular-classroom teachers by illustrating practical suggestions for meeting the needs of special children in their classrooms. Topics include the examination and selection of appropriate materials, the adaptation of available classroom materials, the modification of instructional techniques and tasks, and the evaluation of instruction through classroom observation and various testing procedures.

Hello Everybody. Dr. James Stanfield. 1977. Published by James Stanfield Film Associates, P.O. Box 851, Pasadena, CA 91102. $35.00 per sound filmstrip, $175.00 per set.

The six filmstrips and cassettes, guide, and supplemental materials in this series are designed for students in grades 4-10, parent groups, and teachers. These sound filmstrips introduce six preadolescent and adolescent students, who discuss and illustrate their respective strengths and weaknesses. Students with the following handicaps are highlighted: hearing and speech impairment, visual impairment, orthopedic handicaps, developmental disabilities, learning disabilities, and behavioral disorders.

Education of All Handicapped Act (P.L. 94-142): What It Means to You. P.J. Hancock. 1977. Published by Eye Gate Media, 146-01 Archer Avenue, Jamaica, NY 11435. $24.90 per set. Order number E849.

Two color filmstrips and a cassette briefly present mainstreaming, IEPs, due process, funding, transportation, and architectural considerations. This set is designed for school administrators, support personnel, and parents.

Guide for Trainers: A Resource for Workshops on Developing Individual Education Programs. Arranged and edited by Michael Norman. National Association of State Directors of Special Education. 1977. Published by National Association of State Directors of Special Education (NASDSE), 1201 16th Street, N.W., Washington, DC 20036. $3.00 per copy, or $2.50 each (prepaid) in quantities of 10 or more.

This 152-page trainer's manual provides state and local education-agency personnel with a simulated training process, and materials designed to help planning committees improve their abilities in developing IEPs.

Publisher Source Directory. Staff, NIMIS/NCEMMH and New York State Education Department, 1977. Published by NIMIS/NCEMMH, c/o Publication Sales Division, Ohio State University Press, 2070 Neil Avenue, Columbus, OH 43210. $5.00.

Used in conjunction with the NIMIS bibliographies, this 138-page booklet lists over 1,600 producers of instructional materials and educational aids, devices, and media. Each producer is coded to specify which of the 74 possible formats of educational products it sells or rents.

Instructional Based Appraisal System: Resource Set. Edward L. Meyen, Editor. 1977. Published by Edmark Associates, 13241 Northup Way, Bellevue, WA 98005. $60.00. Product number 151.

This set of materials, including an "Introduction to IBAS," diagnostician's manual, teacher's guide, IBAS management forms, and objective-cluster banks, is designed for managing and planning individual prescriptive programs for handicapped students in reading, mathematics, and social skill/behavior development. This system provides for continuous monitoring of pupil performance, relates appraisal directly to instructional planning, and defines clusters of 224 separate goals and accompanying objectives for the curricular areas above.

Comprehensive Approach to Pupil Planning (CAPP Model). Connecticut State Department of Education, Bureau of Pupil Personnel/Special Educational Services. 1977. Published by Connecticut State Department of Education, Bureau of Pupil Personnel/Special Educational Services, P.O. Box 2219, Hartford, CT 06115. Price available upon request.

This kit contains three manuals, a planning and placement team agenda, classroom support procedures, a teacher's instructional plan form, and six booklets describing research studies conducted under Connecticut Special Act 74-100. An experimental edition of a three-stage model (i.e., classroom support, planning and placement, and instructional planning), the kit not only facilitates educational decision making, but also addresses the following issues: the concept of the least restrictive environment, procedural safeguards, and a free and appropriate education for all handicapped children.

Annotated Index of Tests and Measurements for Teacher and Professional Use in Grades 6-12

appendix E

Achievement Testing
Peabody Individual Achievement Test
Authors. Lloyd M. Dunn & Fredrick C. Markwardt
American Guidance Service, Inc.
Publisher's Bldg.
Circle Pines, MN 55014
This test is not timed. It gives a youngster the opportunity to perform in all areas without pressure of time. The lag in reading will not interfere with a true measure of performance in any area other than Reading Recognition and Reading Comprehension subtests. It must be administered on a one-to-one basis.
Wide Range Achievement Test (WRAT) Jastak
Guidance Associates
1526 Gilpin Avenue
Wilmington, DE 19806
This test is similar in overall intent. There is, however, a written math performance subtest (Levels I and II) and written spelling, and coding subtests. There is no reading comprehension subtest.

Reading Achievement
Gates-MacGinitie Reading Tests: Speed, Vocabulary & Comprehension
Teachers College Press
Columbia University
1234 Amsterdam Ave.
New York, NY 10027
These tests are available at all grade levels from reading readiness through grade 12. They are read by the student, and are subject to time limits. They are appropriate for large- or small-group testing.

229

Gates-McKillop Reading Test
Teachers College Press
Columbia University
1234 Amsterdam Ave.
New York, NY 10027

This is a thorough diagnostic test in the traditional sense. It can be used to determine a student's main area of word-attack and reading errors, and is especially useful for the middle grades (4-7).

Davis Reading Test
Psychological Corporation
304 East 46th Street
New York, NY 10017

This is an excellent traditional test of reading speed and comprehension skills for middle to high school grades. It can be administered in groups large and small.

Auditory Tests
Lindamood Auditory Test (LAC)
Teaching Resources Corporation
100 Boylston Street
Boston, MA 02116

This is a primary test of auditory sequencing.

Tests of Judgment, Reasoning, and Spatial Orientation
Ravens Progressive Matrices
Western Psychological Services
12031 Wilshire Blvd.
Los Angeles, CA 90025

These interesting tests suggest youngsters' (and adults') capacities for observation and reasoned thinking in solving certain visual problems. It gives some insights into the way youngsters handle certain thought processes.

Wide Range Intelligence & Personality Test
Western Psychological Services
12031 Wilshire Blvd.
Los Angeles, CA 90025

This series of tests gives educators a graphic personality-educational profile of secondary-school youngsters with regard to their performance in verbal academic areas, contact with reality, psychomotor efficiency, self-motivated drive. I.Q. number can be derived if desired.

"A Standardized Road-Map Test of Direction Sense"
Johns Hopkins University Press
Baltimore, MD 21218

This is an interesting spatial-directional test appropriate to people ages 7-adult. It is especially helpful in unearthing latent perceptual difficulty in an adolescent long after he has learned spatial and directional problems and gives insight into the kinds of directional orientation problems that may characterize learning style. It is especially helpful in discovering residual symptoms of dyslexia. No special training is necessary to administer the test.

Hooper Visual Organization Test
Western Psychological Services
12031 Wilshire Blvd.
Los Angeles, CA 90025

This is a test of visual organization skills for teenagers and adults.

Visual Motor Integration

Beery-Buktenica Developmental Test of Visual Motor Integration
Bender Gestalt Test
Follett Publications
1010 W. Washington Blvd.
Chicago, IL 60607

These tests give some picture of the way in which a youngster is perceiving, processing what he sees, and reproducing forms in written performance.

Memory for Designs Test
Psychological Test Specialists
P.O. Box 1441
Missoula, MT 59807

In this test the factor of immediate memory enters the test performance. A suggestion of limitations or strength of immediate memory gives a better picture of the student's learning style.

Vocabulary Testing

Peabody Picture Vocabulary Test
American Guidance Service, Inc.
Publisher's Bldg.
Circle Pines, MN 55014

This short, individually administered intelligence and vocabulary test (concept levels) can be used as a screening device. It is especially good for youngsters exhibiting either speech impediments or shyness with regard to verbal expression.

Ammons Full Range Picture Vocabulary Test
Psychological Test Specialists
P.O. Box 1441
Missoula, MT 59807

This test of receptive vocabulary understanding can also produce a limited I.Q. score.

Mathematics Testing

Noonan-Spradley Diagnostic Program of Computational Skills
Allied Educational Council
Distribution Center
P.O. Box 78
Galien, MI 49113

This is a program of testing and basic skills remediation in math. Processes are examined step-by-step and remediated step-by-step. The format is simple and explicit.

Peabody Individual Achievement Test (Mathematics Subtest)
American Guidance Service, Inc.
Publishers Bldg.
Circle Pines, MN 55014

This excellent qualitative analysis of where a youngster's math skills break down is helpful in determining in which areas remediation should be undertaken.

California Algebra Aptitude Test
American Guidance Service, Inc.
Publishers Building
Circle Pines, MN 55014

This is a useful test to determine whether a student is ready and able to begin high school algebra, or whether he needs a thorough remedial math class.

Wide Range Achievement Test (Mathematics Subtest)
Guidance Associates
1526 Gilpin Avenue
Wilmington, DE 19806

Oral Reading Tests

Gilmore Oral Reading Test
Harcourt Brace Jovanovich
757 Third Ave.
New York, NY 10017

This test includes diagnostic information concerning substitutions, mispronunciations, punctuation errors, hesitations, etc., and is a good, quick survey to gain an immediate instructional level (grades 1-10).

Gray Oral Reading Test
Bobbs-Merrill Co., Inc.
4300 West 62nd Street
Indianapolis, IN 46268

This test also reveals immediate instructional level (appropriate material, grades 1-12).

Aptitude Testing
    Detroit Tests of Learning Aptitude
    Bobbs-Merrill Co., Inc.
    4300 West 62nd Street
    Indianapolis, IN 46268
    This is a thorough battery of aptitude tests that yield a student's composite
mental age, as well as a series of subtests that yield his component mental ages. It is
appropriate when strengths and weaknesses need to be ascertained. There are
subtests appropriate to ages 3-6, 6-9, 9-12, and 14 years and older. It must be
administered one-to-one, and requires at least 60 minutes of testing time.
    Verbal Power Test of Concept Equivalents
    Western Psychological Services
    12031 Wilshire Boulevard
    Los Angeles, CA 90025
    This is an interesting test of similarities and differences in language. It is helpful
to gain insight into the college-readiness of high school students (grades 10, 11,
and 12), in that it gives comparative scores for students currently enrolled in
college programs. The high school student may realistically compare his language
sophistication with college students'. It is helpful in motivating college-bound
youngsters to work independently in language development skills prior to college
boards.
    Illinois Index of Scholastic Aptitude (Grades 9-12)
    Western Psychological Services
    12031 Wilshire Blvd.
    Los Angeles, CA 90025
    This is another helpful measure of the language sophistication of the college-
bound youngster in secondary school. It involves use of synonyms, antonyms, and
paragraph comprehension skills. Levels of academic aptitude approximate predictable levels of achievement for a four-year secondary program.

Tests of Phonics & Specific Learning Disability
    Roswell Chall Phonics & Word Analysis Skills
    Essay Press
    Box 5, Planetarium Station
    New York, NY 10024
    This is a very quick, easy-to-administer survey of phonics skills, word attack,
blending, and sound discrimination. Basic rules of syllabification can also be
ascertained. It should be administered one-to-one, and takes five minutes.
    Slingerland Screening Test (Level 6) for Specific Language Disability
    Educators Publishing Services
    75 Moulton Street
    Cambridge, MA 02138

Form C is appropriate for adolescents performing on a fourth- to fifth-grade level. This screening test (for use with groups of five to ten) ascertains areas of strength and weakness in visual recall, auditory discrimination, recall, and written encoding.

Malcomesius Screening Test of Specific Language Disability
Educators Publishing Services
75 Moulton Street
Cambridge, MA 02138

This series of tests is similar to the Slingerland tests. It is particularly geared to adolescents performing at sixth- to eighth-grade levels, but can be used with older students.

Gillingham Phonics Proficiency Scales
Educators Publishing Services
75 Moulton Street
Cambridge, MA 02138

This series of scales of phonics can be used both to test for phonetic problems and to teach phonics.

Tools for Counseling
Vineland Social Maturity Scale
American Guidance Service, Inc.
Publishers Building
Circle Pines, MN 55014

This informal approximation of general social levels — through observation and task analysis of youngsters and young adults, ages 1-24—gives a rough idea of what can be expected socially at each developmental level.

The Forty-Eight Item Counseling Evaluation Test
Western Psychological Services
12031 Wilshire Blvd.
Los Angeles, CA 90025

This test aims at giving the remedial therapist, teacher, or counselor some hint of problem areas within which the adolescent is being subjected to the greatest tensions. Scoring suggests the areas that need either exploration and reexamination or referral for more intensive therapy.

Myklebust Pupil Rating Scale Screening for Learning Disabilities
Grune & Stratton, Inc.
757 Third Avenue
New York, NY 10017

This is an effective tool to separate evaluation of performance into five areas of performance appropriate to success in learning: auditory comprehension, spoken language, orientation, motor coordination, and personal social behavior.

Appendix F

"Know Yourself " Student Inventory*

*Adapted from Introduction to Vocations Manual, New Jersey State Department of Education. Reprinted with permission.

appendix F

Answer "True" or "False" to each of the following questions by circling your choice. (An asterisk indicates the correct answer.)

1. More than 75 percent of the people working are content with their occupations.
   a. True
   *b. False
2. Being able to get along with people is a trait that an individual must have if he hopes to succeed on a job.
   *a. True
   b. False
3. Values are the things we think are important.
   *a. True
   b. False
4. Most people's personalities begin forming after the age of twelve.
   a. True
   *b. False
5. After a person's personality has been formed, it is impossible to change it.
   a. True
   *b. False
6. An interest inventory test will give you your I.Q. score.
   a. True
   *b. False
7. An individual who has great interest in the outdoors might consider a career in forestry or conservation.
   *a. True
   b. False

8. A person who knows and understands his abilities, aptitudes, and interests will be better able to make a career choice than a person who does not have this information.
   *a. True
   b. False
9. A high school education is an important asset for obtaining a job in today's market.
   *a. True
   b. False
10. Lifetime earnings for non-high school graduates are about equal to those of high school graduates.
    a. True
    *b. False
11. The personal appearance of a job applicant is not important to the person conducting the interview.
    a. True
    *b. False
12. Many young people are fearful of going for a job interview.
    *a. True
    b. False

Answer the following questions by circling one or more of the letters on the left.

13. Understanding myself is important because:
    a. it will help me understand myself better
    b. it will help me choose my friends
    c. it will help me plan my life realistically
    *d. all of the above
14. The different cycles in this course will:
    a. help me learn about different types of occupations
    b. teach me how to do better on tests
    c. help me get a part-time job
    *d. all of the above
15. Learning about my interests and aptitudes will:
    a. help make me a better person
    b. help me determine whether or not I should quit school
    c. help me evaluate myself and my plans for the future
    *d. all of the above
16. A personality trait that will help me succeed in a job is:
    a. tardiness
    b. immaturity
    c. laziness
    *d. honesty

17. The purpose of an interest inventory test is:
    a. to learn how smart I am
    b. to determine whether I am capable of going to college
    c. to find a specific job for me
    *d. to determine the types of interests I have, and to relate broad occupational categories to those interests

18. The first things that a person does when applying for a job with a company are to:
    a. take a physical examination
    *b. fill out a job application form
    *c. speak to the personnel manager
    d. demand an interview with the company president

19. Job application forms do not ask questions about:
    a. your hobbies and interests
    b. your career goals
    *c. your religion and ethnic background
    d. your school record and work experience

20. It is important to show up for a job interview looking:
    *a. neatly dressed and well-groomed
    *b. ready for work
    c. very flashy and overly dressed
    d. sleepy-eyed and casually dressed

21. Define the following terms:
    a. aptitude—
    b. interest—
    c. values—
    d. vocations—

22. List four personality traits that you have. [The teacher must decide if a student's answers are "correct."]
    a.
    b.
    c.
    d.

23. List four personality traits that you admire. Explain why. [Have the student use a separate sheet for his answers. The teacher must decide if the student's answers are "correct."]
    a.
    b.
    c.
    d.

24. Name at least four things that you should ask someone about an occupation in which you are interested. [Have the student use a separate sheet for his answers.] Examples of questions you might wish to ask the student:
   a. What are the education requirements?
   b. What is the salary range?
   c. Are there any fringe benefits?
   d. What are the working conditions like?
   e. Is this a job with a future?
25. List four things that you hope to learn from taking this inventory. [Have the student use a separate sheet for his answers. The teacher must decide if the student's answers are "correct."]

Selected Resources for Teachers and Parents Concerned with Learning Disabilities

appendix G

Resources for Teachers

American Vocational Journal (secondary), Vocational Association, Inc., 1510 H Street NW, Washington, D.C. 20005.

Audiovisual Instruction, Association for Educational Communications and Technology, 1201 16th Street NW, Washington, D.C. 20036.

The College Board Review, College Entrance Exam Board, 888 Seventh Avenue, New York, NY 10019.

Education, Project Innovation, 1402 West Capitol Drive, Milwaukee, Wisconsin 53206.

Educational Technology, Educational Technology Publications, Inc., 140 Sylvan Avenue, Englewood Cliffs, New Jersey 07632.

The High School Journal, University of North Carolina Press, University of North Carolina, Bynum Hall, Chapel Hill, North Carolina 27514.

Journal of Reading, International Reading Association, 800 Barksdale Road, Newark, Delaware 19711.

Phi Delta Kappan, Phi Delta Kappa, Eighth Street and Union Avenue, Bloomington, Indiana 47401.

Reading Improvement, Project Innovation, 1402 West Capitol Drive, Milwaukee, Wisconsin 53206.

The School Counselor, American Personnel and Guidance Association, 1607 New Hampshire Avenue NW, Washington, D.C. 20009.

Resources for Parents

Anderson, Laurul E. (Ed by) *Helping the Adolescent with the Hidden Handicap.* Academic Therapy, 1539 Fourth St., San Rafaël, Cal., 1970.

Association for Children with Learning Disabilities, 2200 Brownsville Road, Pittsburgh, Pennsylvania 15210.

Birch, Herbert G. (Ed. by) *Brain Damage in Children.* Association for the Aid of Crippled Children, Williams & Wilkins, 428 E. Preston St., Baltimore, MD 21202, 1964.

Brutten, Milton. *Something's Wrong with My Child.* Harcourt, Brace, Jovanovich, 1973.

Craig, Eleanor. *P.S. You're Not Listening.* NAL, 1301 Ave. of the Americas, New York, NY 10019, 1973.

Ernst, Kenneth. *Games Students Play: And What to Do About Them.* Celestial Arts, 231 Adrian Road, Milbral, Cal. 94030, 1972.

Ginott, Haim. *Between Parent and Teenager.* Avon, 959 Eighth Ave., New York, NY 10017, 1973.

Golic, M. *A Parents Guide to Learning Problems.* Quebec Association for Children with Learning Disability, 6338 Victoria Ave., Montreal 252, Quebec, Canada.

Kronich, Doreen. *They Too Can Succeed: A Practical Guide for Parents of Learning Disabled Children.* Academic Therapy, 1539 Fourth St., San Rafael, Cal. 94907.

McKee, William. *A Primer for Parents.* Houghton Mifflin, NY pamphlet.

Weiss, Helen and Martin. *A Parents, Teachers Guide to Learning Disability.* Center for Educational Services and Research, BOCES, Yorktown, NY 10598, 1973.

Index

Note: Underlined page numbers indicate exhibits or pages including exhibits.

About the Author

DOLORES M. WOODWARD has had extensive experience with "exceptional" populations of adolescents. In addition to teaching she has served as an educational diagnostician, educational director, and school principal. Her accomplishments include the creation of two residential education centers (one a national model) under her educational leadership and guidance. As a graduate level lecturer in special education at Saint Joseph College in Connecticut, she has, for several years, been involved in the training of special educators. Dr. Woodward has served as a consultant to the Connecticut State Department of Education and has presented workshops and in-service training to several school systems throughout Connecticut on mainstreaming.

Residing in Connecticut with her husband and two daughters, Dolores is presently the Assistant Superintendent of Schools for the Special School District of the State of Connecticut, Department of Children and Youth Services.